Handbook on Environmental Due Diligence in Mineral Supply Chains

OECD
BETTER POLICIES FOR BETTER LIVES

This work is published under the responsibility of the Secretary-General of the OECD. The opinions expressed and arguments employed herein do not necessarily reflect the official views of the Member countries of the OECD.

This document, as well as any data and map included herein, are without prejudice to the status of or sovereignty over any territory, to the delimitation of international frontiers and boundaries and to the name of any territory, city or area.

Please cite this publication as:
OECD (2023), *Handbook on Environmental Due Diligence in Mineral Supply Chains*, OECD Publishing, Paris, https://doi.org/10.1787/cef843bf-en.

ISBN 978-92-64-52206-0 (print)
ISBN 978-92-64-72519-5 (pdf)
ISBN 978-92-64-76744-7 (HTML)
ISBN 978-92-64-54035-4 (epub)

Photo credits: © Dmitrii Zotov/Getty Images.

Corrigenda to OECD publications may be found on line at: www.oecd.org/about/publishing/corrigenda.htm.

Foreword

The OECD has been at the forefront of providing guidance on how businesses can maximise their positive contributions to sustainable development through identifying and addressing adverse impacts in their operations and supply chains. This work is rooted in three key OECD instruments that provide government-backed recommendations on responsible business conduct (RBC): the OECD Guidelines for Multinational Enterprises on Responsible Business Conduct (MNE Guidelines), the OECD Due Diligence Guidance for Responsible Business Conduct (RBC Guidance) and, in the minerals sector, the OECD Due Diligence Guidance for Responsible Supply Chains of Minerals from Conflict-Affected and High-Risk Areas (Minerals Guidance). Together, these instruments set out the expectations of governments for enterprises to conduct due diligence to identify, prevent and mitigate actual and potential adverse impacts in mineral supply chains.

The purpose of this Handbook is to support the implementation by business of OECD standards on responsible business conduct by elaborating on how to use the OECD due diligence framework to take account of environmental risks and adverse impacts in mineral supply chains, from extraction to processing, smelting or refining, and recycling. This Handbook is part of the work the OECD undertakes to provide practical support to enterprises on the implementation of standards on RBC risks, an earlier example in the minerals sector being the *Practical actions for companies to identify and address the worst forms of child labour in mineral supply chains*. Beyond the mineral supply chains, the OECD has also developed tailored guidance to help businesses carry out due diligence in other sectors, specifically in the garment and footwear, finance, and agriculture sectors.

Acknowledgements

The project was funded in part by the German Ministry for the Environment, Nature Conservation, Nuclear Safety and Consumer Protection (BMUV). The German Environment Agency (UBA) and the German Federal Institute for Geosciences and Natural Resources (BGR) provided support and assistance.

This Handbook was authored by the OECD Centre for Responsible Business Conduct, which drew on the technical expertise and support of UBA, BGR and OECD's Environment Directorate. Levin Sources Limited provided support in the initial drafting and consultation process. The document also benefitted from input from 25 organisations as part of an expert working group, including representatives from government, the private sector and civil society. The authors would like to gratefully acknowledge the time and valuable input provided by the members of the expert working group. During the development of the Handbook, the OECD Secretariat held several working meetings with experts on artisanal and small-scale mining, remedy, circularity and recycling. In addition, the Secretariat received extensive feedback from industry and civil society as part of an informal public consultation that took place from July to September 2022. Input was also received from Delegates to the OECD Working Party on Responsible Business Conduct (WPRBC). The Secretariat would like to thank all of those who dedicated their time and shared their knowledge as part of these processes.

Table of contents

FIGURES

TABLES

Executive summary

Enterprises play a key role in advancing sustainable economies and can contribute to delivering an effective and progressive response to global, regional and local environmental challenges, including the urgent threat of climate change. The upstream segment of the mineral supply chain (generally understood as the point of extraction through to the point of transformation) has traditionally been associated with significant environmental risks and impacts. At the same time, the sector is growing, driven by an increasing demand for minerals to fulfil the material needs of a growing and increasingly affluent global population, as well as ambitious government and business renewable energy targets and rising demand for minerals critical to the energy and digital transition, such as cobalt, copper, lithium, nickel and rare earths among others.[1] Although a more 'circular economy' based on recycling and reuse of minerals has clear potential for reducing certain environmental risks and adverse impacts, primary extraction of minerals will remain critical to delivering the low carbon transition and more broadly achieving the Sustainable Development Goals (SDGs) at the speed required.[2]

This Handbook provides an introduction to environmental issues in the upstream segment of mineral supply chains. It is intended to help downstream enterprises (metal traders and exchanges, component manufacturers, product manufacturers, original equipment manufacturers and retailers) understand how they can embed environmental considerations into their supply chain due diligence processes, while also helping upstream enterprises (miners, local traders and exporters, international concentrate traders, smelters and refiners, and recyclers[3]) meet the due diligence expectations of their customers and other downstream business relationships.

The Handbook has four sections. **Chapter 1** provides the background on why risk-based environmental due diligence matters to businesses operating in mineral supply chains and considers environmental due diligence in the context of two important topics in the minerals sector: artisanal and small-scale mining (ASM) and circular value chain approaches. **Chapter 2** clarifies what is meant by adverse environmental impacts and provides examples of common environmental issues found in upstream mineral supply chains. It also aims to help businesses understand factors that may affect the severity and likelihood of environmental risks. **Chapter 3** discusses integrating environmental risks and impacts into enterprises' implementation of the OECD six-step due diligence framework and finally **Chapter 4** leads readers through the six-step risk-based due diligence framework, answering specific questions on how business can address environmental considerations under each of the steps. Annex A includes a Glossary of environmental terms while Annex B provides a, non-comprehensive, list of useful resources and materials.

1 Introduction

This introduction sets out why risk-based environmental due diligence matters to businesses operating in mineral supply chains and considers environmental due diligence in the context of two important topics in the minerals sector: artisanal and small-scale mining (ASM) and circular value chain approaches.

Why environmental due diligence matters to businesses operating in mineral supply chains

Enterprises play a key role in advancing sustainable economies and can contribute to delivering an effective and progressive response to global, regional and local environmental challenges, including contributing to reaching the goals of climate change mitigation and adaptation. Meanwhile, environmental degradation presents risks to people and the planet that may be heightened by business activities. Expectations for environmental action by the private sector have been spurred by public policy, civil society, the scientific community, investors and industry itself, with public pressure and litigation playing an important role.[4] Nationally Determined Contributions (NDCs) include the objective to mobilize finance flows towards low greenhouse gas (GHG) and climate-resilient development and recognise non-party stakeholders, including business, as an integral part of the global solution (United Nations Framework Convention on Climate Change, 2016[1]).[5]

Increasing demand for minerals to fulfil the material needs of a growing and increasingly affluent global population (OECD, 2019[2]),[6] renewable energy targets and demand for minerals such as cobalt, copper and lithium for the energy and digital transitions is driving growth in the mining and metals sector. Although a more 'circular economy' based on recycling and reuse of minerals has clear potential for reducing certain environmental risks and adverse impacts, primary extraction of minerals will remain critical to delivering the low-carbon transition and, more broadly, achieving the Sustainable Development Goals (SDGs).[7] There is an insufficient amount of metals currently in circulation for the deployment of low-carbon technologies at a scale consistent with agreed climate targets, and therefore continued mineral extraction is needed (IEA, 2021[3]).

Identifying and addressing adverse environmental impacts in the upstream segment, where this primary mineral extraction takes place, may help an enterprise maximise positive contributions to society and sustainable development, improve stakeholder relationships, protect its reputation, and create more value by reducing operational costs by, for example, finding ways to use less water or energy. Due diligence processes can also help prevent supply chain blockages and delays, and reduce the time it takes to bring new assets onstream, which is of critical importance when delivering the digital and low-carbon energy transitions. Comprehensive due diligence processes can also help an enterprise meet legal requirements on labour, environmental, corporate governance and anti-bribery requirements.

The respect for and fulfilment of the human right to a clean and healthy environment has been recognised in resolution 48/13 of the UN's Human Rights Council.[8] An enterprise will need to understand the links between environmental and human rights risks in the minerals sector and how to make use of due diligence processes – often already used for human rights risks – when addressing environmental risk and vice versa. Once environmental risks and adverse impacts have been identified, an enterprise should consider the ways in which they generate human rights risks and adverse impacts and ensure any mitigation or remedy addresses both categories. Recognising human rights to a clean and healthy environment is particularly important in ensuring a *just* transition to global net-zero emissions and continued responsible engagement rather than disengagement as the primary approach to environmental risk management in supply chains.

Circularity and enhanced use of secondary resources

As stated above, the demand for minerals and metals to support a growing, low-carbon, global economy over the coming decades cannot be met by one type of source alone. Both primary (mined) and secondary (re-used, refurbished, remanufactured, recycled, recovered) materials will be critical to achieving the clean energy and digital transition. This Handbook therefore promotes RBC in mining, recycling, and minerals and metals processing, all of which will be critical for sustainable development.[9]

Box 1. The circular economy

Although there is no one accepted definition of the circular economy, a circular economy seeks to: (i) maximise the value of the materials and products circulating within the economy; (ii) minimise material consumption, with particular attention to virgin materials, hazardous substances, and certain waste streams (such as plastics, food, electric and electronic goods); (iii) prevent the generation of waste; and (iv) reduce hazardous components in both waste and products (OECD, 2020[4]; OECD, 2021[5]).

In pursuing a circular economy, there are a variety of mechanisms that can modify the flow of products and materials through the economy, and ultimately result in lower rates of natural resource extraction. The OECD has highlighted three main mechanisms including:

- Closing resource loops – the diversion of waste from disposal and subsequent transformation into secondary raw materials.
- Slowing resource loops or flows – the retention of products, and their constituent materials, in the economy for longer periods.
- Narrowing resource flows – generating additional economic value from a fixed amount of natural resources (OECD, 2019[6]).

Source: OECD (2021[7]), The role of OECD instruments on responsible business conduct in progressing environmental objectives, https://mneguidelines.oecd.org/The-role-of-OECD-instruments-on-responsible-business-conduct-in-progressing-environmental-objectives.pdf .

The application of circular economy principles and the use of secondary materials can contribute to the reduction of environmental impacts (Bibas, Chateau and Lanzi, 2021[8]; OECD, 2019[2]). Downstream businesses, as well as upstream businesses like smelters or refiners, may consider where opportunities exist to implement circular economy principles in the design, production, remanufacturing, distribution, consumption, and collection of their products and how these opportunities may be integrated into their business model. Circular economy principles need to be scaled-up and enhanced in mineral supply chains so that materials can be more efficiently and routinely collected and recovered from end-of-life products. Sourcing from secondary materials to complement or replace primary raw materials can offer opportunities to reduce environmental harms if secondary materials or energy from secondary materials are sourced responsibly.

The availability of recycled materials on the market depends on the availability of materials that could be recycled but also on their actual recycling rates (which depend on the technologies currently in place, the economic case for recycling them, regulation in place, etc.) and materials from the 'urban mine' (in-use material stocks), which only become available after a time lag (IEA, 2021[3]). For bulk metals, recycling practices are well established and metals are readily available, but this is not yet the case for many energy transition metals such as lithium and rare earth elements. Emerging waste streams from clean energy technologies (e.g. batteries and wind turbines) are expected to increase after 2030, at a time when mineral demand is set to still be growing rapidly. The IEA estimate that by 2040, recycled quantities of copper, lithium, nickel and cobalt from spent batteries could reduce combined primary supply requirements for these minerals by around 10% (IEA, 2021[3]).

Recycling will not eliminate the need for continued investment in primary supply of minerals and according to the World Bank, investment in primary supply will still be needed even in the case that recycling rates reach 100% by 2050 (World Bank, 2020[9]). Therefore, the Handbook recognises the role of both primary and secondary supply chains in sustainable development, but also notes that, if poorly managed, both can cause environmental risks and impacts. It is important to note that although primary mining in general has more environmental risks than recycling, it can hold significant economic opportunity for regions with high mineral endowments (and in some localities, the only economic opportunity), provided there is good governance and equitable distribution of benefits to the state, local communities, and investors.

Sourcing from Artisanal and Small-Scale Mining

One of the overarching objectives of OECD RBC instruments is the sustainable development of mining communities through responsible engagement, including in high-risk and conflict-affected areas where many producers may be informal. While ASM presents some unique risks, avoiding it altogether instead of seeking to address those risks typically only worsens conditions for mineral-producing communities.

ASM is a source of livelihoods and employment in many regions of the world. It is estimated that ASM employs between 40 and 100 million people worldwide, compared to 7 million in industrial mining (IGF, 2017[10]). Besides being a major source of employment in many developing countries, ASM can also help address security of supply issues for critical minerals, including those key to driving the green transition (Moore et al., 2020[11]).

In many countries, ASM takes place in a regulatory grey zone, whereby its economic role is not explicitly recognised and facilitated by the state, including being properly legislated or regulated, but is largely tolerated. The Minerals Guidance encourages businesses to engage with 'legitimate ASM' and provides a framework for doing so. This framework is elaborated on in the OECD FAQ on Sourcing Gold from Artisanal and Small-Scale Miners (OECD, 2016[12])

Responsible engagement of ASM producers can lead to the progressive formalisation of ASM activities. Formalised mine sites are more capable of working through formal channels of trade, implementing risk management plans, and appear to be subject to more regulatory inspection visits regarding environment, waste management, and radioactivity. In view of these considerations, this Handbook recommends that businesses and other stakeholders seek to engage with legitimate ASM producers in a spirit of progressive improvement, including by considering the provision of technical and financial support to help ASM actors implement corrective action plans. To channel this support, there are several industry-led or multi-stakeholder collaboration and cost sharing mechanisms already in place, and there is the potential for others to be developed.[10]

2 Understanding environmental risks and impacts

This chapter clarifies what is meant by environmental risks and impacts and provides examples of common environmental issues found in upstream mineral supply chains. The Chapter also helps business understand factors that may affect the severity and likelihood of risks, both of which are critical considerations when conducting risk-based due diligence.

What does the Handbook cover?

This Handbook considers a range of environmental risks and impacts that may arise in minerals supply chains from the point of extraction through key points of transformation, primarily mining, smelting, refining, and recycling, for all minerals and metals (whether for domestic or export markets), including construction materials, industrial minerals, base metals, precious metals, gemstones and technology critical elements, amongst others (OECD, 2021[13])). They also recognise that environmental impacts can be collective and interlinked or isolated, as well as localised or transboundary in nature.

The Handbook focuses on the following adverse environmental impacts in mineral supply chains:[11]

- climate change
- biodiversity loss and degradation,[12] covering species and terrestrial, marine and other aquatic ecosystems (for example, deforestation, damage to protected areas and soil erosion)
- air, water and soil pollution
- mismanagement of waste, including hazardous substances
- noise and vibration
- damage to aesthetics and cultural heritage sites
- water depletion.

Given the broad range of environmental risks and adverse impacts that can arise from upstream activities in mineral supply chains, and the various ways that these may manifest in different contexts, this Handbook does not aim to be exhaustive and does not provide extensive detail for each environmental risk area. Instead, it considers examples and points readers to additional resources that may provide further technical information on best practice for assessing, preventing, mitigating and remediating environmental risks and adverse impacts along mineral supply chains.

Box 2. Different ways that environmental impacts may arise and manifest

Potential environmental impacts in minerals supply chains can be understood in a number of ways:

Impacts that result directly by an entity's operational practices. For instance, when a business clears an area resulting in loss of biodiversity (for example forests, wetlands, coral reefs), or when a mine discharges toxic waste resulting in air, water or soil contamination, Impacts can happen:

- Locally (for example mining-related discharge of acid and metalliferous drainage affecting local areas, or a gold processor burning mercury from an amalgam and contaminating downwind areas).
- Remotely (for example continuous discharge of high volumes of air pollutants by a smelter causing remote acid rain, or riverine tailings disposal – when mine tailings are transported over long distances in rivers and sediment deposition causes impacts far downstream).

Impacts that are enabled by, but not a direct result of, an entity's operational practices,[13] for instance:

- When investing in a steel plant, members of the board vote against installing costly equipment which treats run-off from the plant which pollutes local water sources.
- When opening up roads in previously inaccessible areas that attract other economic actors who go on to cause environmental impacts (for example clearing primary or secondary forest).

Impacts that are cumulative and collective in nature. Combined impacts on the environment of more than one activity, that can take place over a period of time (cumulative) or concurrently by several actors (collective), where the aggregate impact can be greater than the individual activities.

- For example, miners and farmers in the same area having a collective impact on a forest, or different mining operators in the same watershed intensifying disturbance of aquatic ecosystems, or the air emissions of multiple refiners reducing air quality within an airshed, or when a smelter or refiner produces GHGs through consumption of fossil fuels in a manner not consistent with internationally agreed global temperature goals (IFC, 2013[14]).

Impacts that have chronic, persistent or constantly recuring adverse consequences for human or ecological systems over a long period of time:

- For example, large-scale consumption of water resulting in water scarcity and localised aquatic ecosystem impacts.

Impacts that are permanent or irreversible, and continue or endure without fundamental or marked change, an impact that cannot be remediated:

- For example, the deforestation of primary rainforest or activities that cause the extinction of a particular species.

Impacts that are acute and occur over a short period of time. They are used to describe brief exposures and effects which appear promptly after exposure:

- For example, tailings dam failure that results in significant and immediate harm to the local environment and communities.

The MNE Guidelines provide specific recommendations for understanding and assessing environmental impacts associated with an enterprise's operations, products and services (see Box 3 below).

What is meant by environmental risks and adverse impacts and how should enterprises assess severity?

For many enterprises, the term *risk* implies financial, market, operational or reputational risk to the enterprise itself. In contrast, the MNE Guidelines refer to risks to people, the environment and society that enterprises cause, contribute to, or to which they are directly linked – an outward-facing approach to risk.

To assess the severity of an environmental impact, businesses should consider the scale, scope and irremediable character of the impact (see Table 1 below for examples of scale, scope and irremediable nature of the impact in the context of environmental impacts).[14]

Table 1. Examples of indicators of scale, scope and irremediable character for adverse environmental impacts

Adverse impact	Examples of scale	Examples of scope	Examples of the irremediable character
Biodiversity loss (e.g. deforestation, coral reef degradation, species loss) and damage to protected areas Climate change / GHG emissions Improper use and disposal of hazardous materials	Extent of impact on human health Extent of changes in species composition Water use intensity (% use of total available resources)	Geographic reach of the impact Number of species impacted	Degree to which rehabilitation of the natural site is possible or practicable The length of time remediation would take

Adverse impact	Examples of scale	Examples of scope	Examples of the irremediable character
Noise and vibration Physical instability, soil erosion and land degradation Pollution (air, water etc) Damage to aesthetics and cultural heritage sites Waste mismanagement Water depletion	Degree of waste and chemical generation (tons; % of generation)		

Source: Adapted from the OECD (2018[15]), OECD Due Diligence Guidance for Responsible Business Conduct, https://mneguidelines.oecd.org/OECD-Due-Diligence-Guidance-for-Responsible-Business-Conduct.pd.f

For example, factors that may influence the severity and likelihood of adverse impacts to the environment in upstream mineral supply chains may include the:

- local environment (e.g. areas of high biodiversity, its proximity to protected areas or world heritage sites)
- vulnerability of the ecosystem and surrounding communities (e.g. water scarce regions)
- material characteristics (e.g. hazard classification, persistence within the environment)
- prevalence of extreme events (e.g. drought, earthquakes)
- political interference, corruption, instability or conflict
- financial viability of the mining operation (e.g. level and type of capitalisation)
- size and scale of operation
- level of organisation/formalisation of the operation
- ownership of the operation (e.g. publicly listed, private, state owned)
- appropriate nature of the technology being used (fit-for-purpose)
- stage of the mining lifecycle (e.g. exploration, post closure)
- level of mechanisation.

Many environmental impacts can lead to impacts on human rights, particularly impacts on human health and safety. This includes, for example, unprotected contact with toxic substances throughout the mining, processing and recycling process and contamination of sources of food and water.

While some environmental impacts will manifest immediately, others will take time – future environmental impacts of certain activities may not be immediately apparent and therefore may be harder to assess and manage, and it may be harder to determine causation. Environmental impacts may also range from short-term (reducing once the cause is removed) to permanent (continuing after the cause is removed).

Table 2. Examples of environmental issues in upstream mineral supply chains

Environmental issue	Description
Biodiversity loss (e.g. deforestation, coral reef degradation, species loss) and damage to protected areas	Biodiversity loss or degradation, of a specific area, for example deforestation and land use change related to open pit mining or damage to marine habitats / ecosystems associated with deep sea mining. It is of high concern for all enterprises operating in forested, marine and other key biodiversity or protected areas, in all stages of the supply chain.
Climate change (e.g. GHG emissions, failure to adapt to	Changes in global temperatures and weather patterns resulting from anthropogenic GHG emissions. GHG emissions in mineral supply chains may be particularly prevalent at the smelting and processing stages of the supply chain. GHG emissions should be measured either on an absolute or intensity basis for scopes 1,2 and 3, where appropriate.[15] As the world is already experiencing climate change – including changes in average temperature, increased frequency

Environmental issue	Description
physical risks of climate change)	of extreme weather events, and changes in seasons – adaptation refers to adjustments in ecological, social or economic systems in response to actual or expected climatic changes. Failure to adapt increases the likelihood of potential damages to the environment, people and society from climate change.
Improper use or disposal of hazardous materials	Materials that when released to the environment, can pose a risk to workers, communities, water sources and wildlife. Examples of hazardous materials include: • elements present in the ore, such as radioisotopes, arsenic, mercury and other heavy metals that are released through minerals processing • process chemicals, such as acids, organic compounds, cyanide and mercury • recycling residues, which may be non-valuable residues or waste containing non-recoverable valuable materials (such as residual lead in wastes from lead-acid battery recycling).
Noise and vibration	Noise and vibrations can disturb and have severe adverse impacts on local biodiversity as well as people. Noise sources include drilling and blasting, fixed and mobile equipment, excavators, the loading/unloading and movement of trucks, crushers, mills, air fans, diesel generators and large or handheld pneumatic, percussion and grinding tools. Vibrations are principally associated with blasting and passage of heavy vehicles.
Physical instability, soil erosion and land degradation	Movement and collapse of tailings storage facilities, waste rock dumps and slopes can remain a risk to local communities and nature over an extended period, including beyond the life of the producing facility. Compaction, extraction and disruption of soil physical structure.
Pollution (air, water etc.)	Contamination of the environment by any chemical, physical or biological agent that modifies the natural characteristics. Planned or accidental discharge of effluents containing physical, chemical and/or biological contaminants into waterbodies, which causes damage to aquatic ecosystems and terrestrial organisms using that water. The risk of water pollution is influenced by site-specific factors, such as rainfall, type of ore being exploited, chemicals being used, sensitivity of the receiving environment and the quality of environmental management. Water pollution is an environmental impact which intersects with the human right of access to safe, affordable and reliable drinking water. Air pollutants include dust, particulates, fumes, vapours and other non-GHG emissions arising from activities such as drilling, blasting, excavation, material size reduction, loading and movement and smelting, refining and recycling. They should be considered in terms of their volumes, treatments and emission locations. Some emissions cause adverse impacts on land and soil quality and ecosystem and human health in downwind areas when particulates and gases are washed out by rainfall or settle under gravity.
Damage to aesthetics and cultural heritage sites	Operations result in visible deterioration and negative aesthetic quality of natural and manmade landscapes or damage to cultural heritage sites, which impairs people's ability to enjoy and benefit from their environment. This typically occurs in circumstances where facilities occupy large land surface areas or where industrial buildings are visible in residential and rural landscapes.
Waste mismanagement	The impact of solid and liquid waste on the environment and human health depends on its hazardous (or non-hazardous) properties, mass and volume and on quality of waste management (collection and treatment). Large volumes of waste can be generated at all stages of the supply chain, but are more prominent where product to waste ratio is low (e.g. low ore grade mining operations) circular regenerative processes are not applied, in upstream operations generally and in recycling operations that do not manage non-valuable materials and hazardous fractions and residues. Waste mismanagement can result in the dispersion of contamination and adversely impact water, soil and air quality.
Water depletion	More water being used than is available by natural replenishment or when water is diverted from ecosystems and users. Risks are often higher in permanent or seasonally arid environments.

Note: Further iterations of this table are provided in Chapter 4: Six step due diligence approach and provide guidance on indicators and sources of information for environmental risks and monitoring of mitigation efforts.

3 Due diligence as a tool

This chapter introduces due diligence as a tool and explains why a risk-based due diligence approach is critical when addressing environmental risks and adverse impacts in businesses own operations and global supply chains.

Risk-based due diligence to address environmental risks and adverse impacts

Risk-based due diligence expects enterprises to identify, prevent, mitigate and account for how they address actual and potential impacts to people, society and the planet. As it will often not be possible for enterprises to identify and respond to all risks and impacts related to their activities and business relationships simultaneously and with the same degree of attention, the MNE Guidelines encourage them to **prioritise their most significant (i.e. severe[16] and likely) risks and impacts,** and to dedicate attention and resources accordingly. In this way, risk-based due diligence is concerned with making progress on the most significant impacts to people, planet and society.

Contextual factors, such as resource availability, availability of data and technologies, firm size, the degree of leverage an enterprise has over a particular supplier, where risks or impacts occur in the supply chain may influence what actions are appropriate in a specific context. The size or resource capacity of an enterprise and the degree of leverage it has over a particular supplier does not change its responsibility to conduct due diligence commensurate with the risk but may affect how an enterprise carries out its due diligence.

Adverse environmental impacts are often closely inter-linked with other matters covered by the MNE Guidelines such as human rights, impacts to workers and communities, access to livelihoods and land tenure rights. In this respect, it is important for enterprises to assess and address **social impacts** in the context of their environmental management and due diligence activities; including as part of their risk prioritisation processes.

Risk-based due diligence not only helps ensure that the most significant adverse impacts are addressed first, it also helps ensure that due diligence is **practically implementable for businesses**. Given the widespread and dispersed nature of environmental impacts in mineral supply chains, enterprises will not be able to identify and respond to every adverse impact, monitor and track every business partner or trace every product simultaneously. As such, a risk-based approach does not expect perfect results or risk-free value chains and does not penalize businesses for the presence of risks or adverse impacts in their supply chains. Instead, it expects enterprises to prioritise appropriately, target their highest risk operations and business relationships and demonstrate meaningful and measurable progress over time against specific, time-bound targets and indicators.

Despite the flexibility provided in the risk-based approach, enterprises are not expected to decide arbitrarily what is and is not important in a specific context. Instead, OECD RBC standards set important parameters for how businesses should prioritise. **Demonstrating credible prioritisation processes and progress against outcome-oriented and time-bound targets** helps to ensure that businesses arrive at decisions about allocating resources and time in a way that is efficient, effective and aligned with international standards.

Due diligence should also be adapted to the nature, severity and likelihood of the adverse impact. When the likelihood and severity of a risk or impact is high, due diligence should be more extensive. This also involves **tailoring approaches to specific risks and impacts**.

The expectation that businesses prioritise risks and impacts based on severity and likelihood **applies to the entire six-step due diligence process** –starting with the high-level scoping of risk issues that then informs the deeper-dive assessments on higher-risk business relationships, through to how an enterprise responds to actual or potential adverse impacts. It also shapes how businesses are expected to track and report on their due diligence.[17]

Target audience and responsibility for due diligence

Due diligence is a whole-of-supply chain process and applies to all business relationships, including those relationships beyond contractual, 'first tier' or immediate relationships (OECD, 2023[16]). Accordingly, all businesses along the minerals supply chain, from the point of extraction to end-user, have a role to play. The nature of due diligence, however, can be affected by a business' position in the supply chain. In supply chains with key points of transformation like smelters and refiners in the minerals sector, OECD standards on RBC recognise the unique role played by such entities as "control points". Downstream enterprises, for example, can make use of control points' leverage and visibility over other suppliers by checking to make sure that control points are conducting due diligence themselves, in order to identify, prevent and mitigate risks at more remote tiers of their supply chain further upstream.

The concept of control points helps delineate responsibilities between upstream entities (miners, local traders and exporters, international concentrate traders, smelters, refiners and recyclers) and downstream entities (metal traders and exchanges, component manufacturers, product manufacturers, original equipment manufacturers and retailers) in many mineral supply chains. The position of control points between downstream enterprises and suppliers further upstream can also influence enterprises' relationships to adverse impacts and thus where the primary responsibility for addressing the impact lies (see Figure 1).

Since this Handbook addresses adverse environmental impacts in the minerals sector from the point of extraction through to key points of transformation, downstream enterprises can use the Handbook *both* to: (a) evaluate the due diligence practices of control points on environmental risks and impacts further upstream; *and* (b) identify and assess impacts at the control point. Control points like smelters and refiners, and other upstream entities should, in turn, exercise leverage over their suppliers to address environmental risks and impacts, in addition to addressing impacts they themselves cause or contribute to.

This Handbook is therefore addressed to all enterprises in mineral supply chains which may be causing, contributing or directly linked to actual or potential adverse environmental impacts. However, it will likely be most useful for enterprises who determine that they are either contributing to or directly linked to environmental risks or impacts in the supply chain. Figure 1 illustrates how entities along mineral supply chains should take account of these concepts in determining the nature of their due diligence. Enterprises using this Handbook are encouraged to bear this in mind and to adapt their due diligence to their position in the supply chain. In addition, the section on integrating environmental considerations into each due diligence step provides several examples of ways in which an entity's position in the mineral supply chain and its relationship to an adverse impact may affect their due diligence.

The OECD Guidelines for Multinational Enterprises on Responsible Business Conduct ("OECD MNE Guidelines") set out expectations on how enterprises should avoid and address adverse environmental impacts related to an enterprise's operations, products and services. An enterprise's relationship to the impact (causing, contributing to, or being directly linked to it) will determine how an enterprise should respond to identified risks. **While many of the risks and mitigation measures in this handbook will be relevant for enterprises seeking to address adverse impacts they cause, this document focusses primarily on due diligence of environmental risks in mineral supply chains, with an emphasis, accordingly, on relationships of contributing or being directly linked to adverse environmental impacts.** Figure 1 illustrates how these relationships may pertain to a typical mineral supply chain. The diagram also reflects the unique role of smelters and refiners as a control point in mineral supply chains, with practical implications for the respective roles of downstream entities and upstream entities based on the OECD Due Diligence Guidance for Responsible Supply Chains of Minerals from Conflict-Affected and High-Risk Areas.

Figure 1. Addressing environmental impacts in mineral supply chains

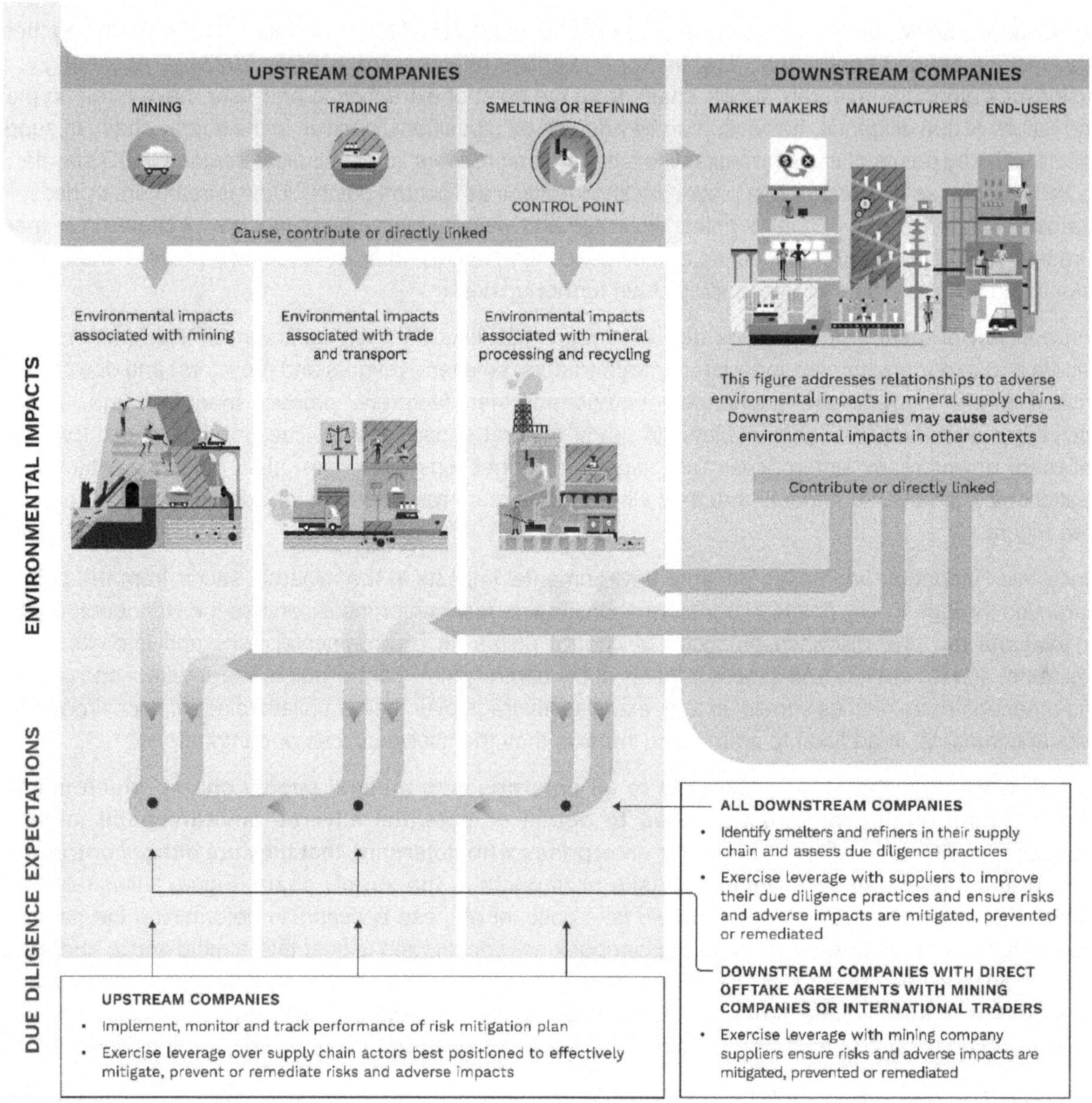

This Handbook may also be useful for other parties, such as sector-wide and multi-stakeholder initiatives that facilitate collaboration on due diligence activities, and for workers, trade unions and workers' representatives, and civil society organisations, including environmental human rights defenders.

Box 3. Cause, contribute and directly linked in the context of environmental impacts

The cause, contribute and directly linked concepts, established in the RBC Guidance, provide a framework for understanding a business relationship to an actual or potential impact to determine the appropriate responses.

The MNE Guidelines set out expectations on how enterprises should avoid and address adverse environmental impacts and contribute to reaching the goals of climate change mitigation and adaptation; the conservation, restoration, and sustainable use of biological diversity; the sustainable, efficient and lawful use of land, resources and energy; sustainable consumption and production including through promotion of circular economy approaches; and pollution prevention, reduction and control.

The Guidelines define adverse environmental impacts as "significant changes in the environment or biota which have harmful effects on the composition, resilience, productivity or carrying capacity of natural and managed ecosystems, or on the operation of socio-economic systems or on people" and note that environmental impacts should be assessed in light of best available science.

Under the MNE Guidelines an enterprise "**causes**" an adverse environmental impact if its activities on their own are sufficient to result in the adverse impact. An enterprise "**contributes** to" an adverse environmental impact if its activities, in combination with the activities of other entities cause the impact, or if the activities of the enterprise cause, facilitate or incentivise another entity to cause an adverse impact. Adverse environmental impacts can also be "**directly linked"** to an enterprise's business operations, products or services by a business relationship, even if they do not contribute to those impacts". Under OECD RBC standards, contribution must be substantial, meaning that it does not include minor or trivial contributions. The RBC Guidance provides additional guidance on these terms.

Environmental impacts can be collective and interlinked or isolated; they can also be localised or transboundary in nature. While some environmental impacts are well understood, the extent, nature and cause of others may be less well understood, evolving, or even unknown. Therefore, while in some instances it will be possible to assess, based on available science and information, to what extent an enterprise is contributing to an adverse environmental impact, in other instances such an assessment may be challenging. In the context of the latter situation, for the purposes of the MNE Guidelines, the assessment of an enterprise's contribution to adverse impacts should consider the extent to which its activities are consistent with widely recognised standards, environmental management processes and safeguards regarding good environmental practice; benchmarks and standards established in applicable environmental rules and regulatory frameworks; and relevant international agreements.

Source: OECD (2023[16]), *OECD Guidelines for Multinational Enterprises on Responsible Business Conduct*, https://doi.org/10.1787/81f92357-en.

This Handbook demonstrates how existing OECD instruments, namely the Due Diligence Guidance for Responsible Business Conduct (RBC Guidance) and the Due Diligence Guidance for Responsible Supply Chains of Minerals from Conflict-Affected and High-Risk Areas (Minerals Guidance), can be used to address environmental risks and impacts in the minerals sector. It does so by situating existing recommendations in a relevant context, providing examples of how they can be applied and directing users to related resources. It does not provide new recommendations or risk management expectations.

Figure 2. How to use OECD instruments on RBC together

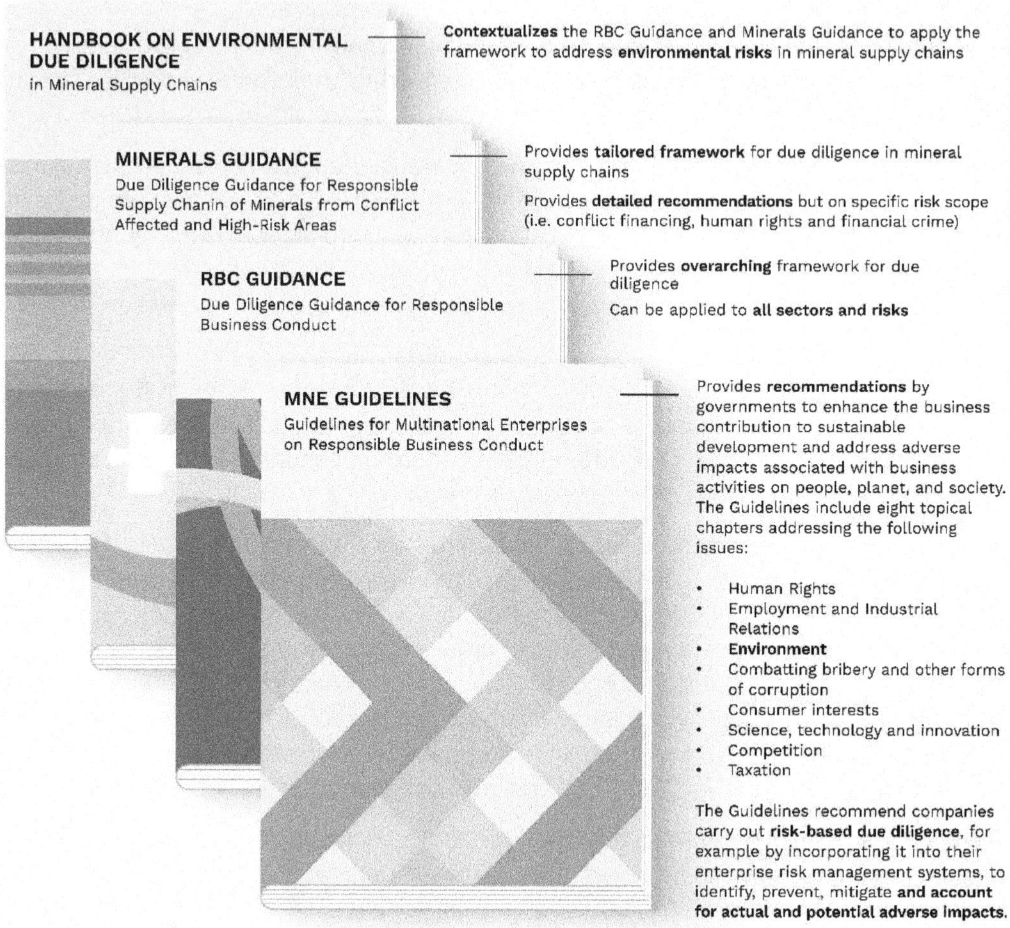

The OECD Guidelines for Multinational Enterprises on Responsible Business Conduct (MNE Guidelines) are the only comprehensive set of government-backed expectations on how business address adverse impacts on people and the environment. The OECD has developed specific due diligence guidance covering different sectors of the economy (e.g. in mineral, garment and agriculture supply chains) and on specific issues like stakeholder engagement in the extractive sector. In 2018, the OECD developed the sector-agnostic Guidance for RBC that draws from and builds on sector specific guidance but applies to businesses in all sectors of the economy. Figure 2 provides illustrates how various OECD instruments on RBC can be used together.

4 Six step due diligence approach

This chapter leads readers through the six-step risk-based due diligence framework, answering specific questions on how business can address environmental considerations under each of the steps.

Integrating environmental risk management into due diligence systems

This Handbook is addressed to all businesses in the minerals supply chain. However, as businesses have different responsibilities depending on their relationship to identified risks and impacts, they will use the information provided in this Chapter in different ways – depending on their position in the supply chain and on their size, where their most significant environmental risks lie, the nature, severity and likelihood of the impacts they face in practice and the nature of their business relationships.

Figure 3. Due diligence process and supporting measures

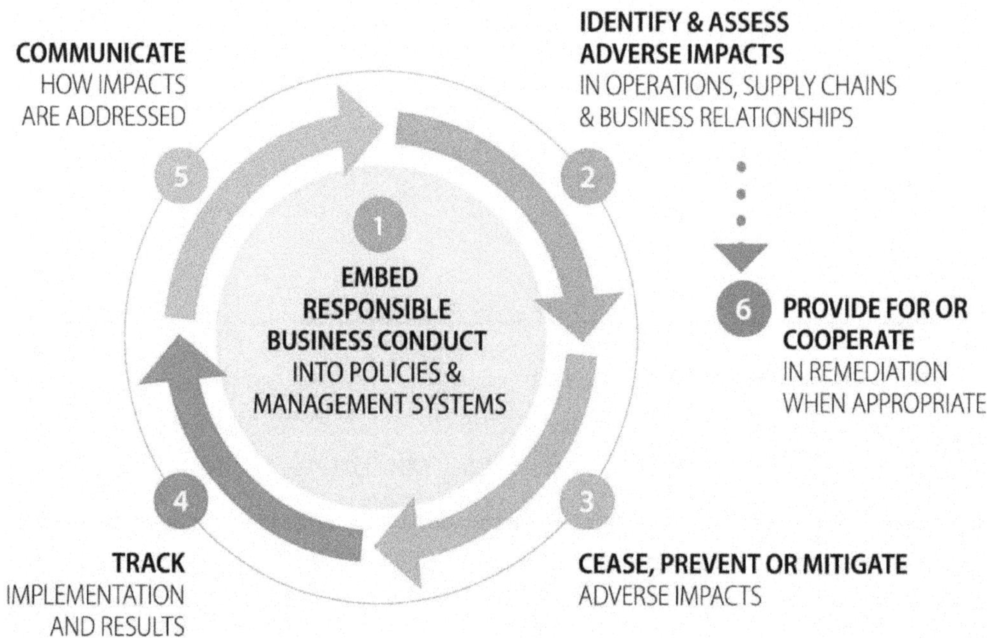

Source: OECD (2018[15]), OECD Due Diligence Guidance for Responsible Business Conduct, https://mneguidelines.oecd.org/OECD-Due-Diligence-Guidance-for-Responsible-Business-Conduct.pdf.

Step 1: Embed RBC into policies and management systems

What do the RBC Guidance and Minerals Guidance say?

- **Devise, adopt and disseminate a policy – or combination of policies – on RBC issues** that articulate the enterprise's commitments to the principles and standards contained in the MNE Guidelines and its plans for implementing due diligence, for the enterprise's own operations, its supply chain and other business relationships.
- **Embed the enterprise's policies on RBC issues into oversight bodies and management systems** so that they are implemented as part of the regular business processes, and **incorporate RBC expectations and policies into engagement with suppliers** and other business relationships.
- Establish a **system of controls and transparency** over the mineral supply chain. This includes a chain of custody or a traceability system or the identification of upstream actors in the supply chain.

Key questions on how to integrate environmental risk considerations into Step 1:

- 1.1 How can an enterprise integrate environmental risk considerations into RBC policies and management systems?
- 1.2 How can an enterprise ensure that its RBC policies are fit for purpose and progressively tailor them to the enterprise's most severe and likely risks (identified under Step 2)?
- 1.3 What is the relationship between existing environmental management systems (EMS) and environmental due diligence under OECD RBC standards?

1.1 How can an enterprise integrate environmental risk considerations into RBC policies and management systems?

The first step in integrating an enterprise's most significant environmental risks into RBC policies and management systems is to identify and prioritise the broad categories of environmental risks the due diligence system will seek to manage and why.

Enterprises should review and update their existing policies to align with the principles and standards of the MNE Guidelines, and can consider developing specific policies on their most significant environmental risks –building on findings from their scoping, assessment and prioritisation processes under Step 2. They should also update their due diligence policy commitments as risks in the supply chain emerge and evolve. Table 2. provides an indicative non-exhaustive list of some environmental issues in upstream mineral supply chains that enterprises can consider integrating into their policies and management systems (and, where relevant, consider when reviewing a supplier's own due diligence practices under Step 2).

As part of putting in place RBC due diligence policy and management systems, enterprises should also take proportionate, risk-based steps to:

- **Understand the enterprise's own capacity, expertise and resources** to collect information and embed due diligence effectively for priority environmental risk issues, with the aim of progressively improving systems and processes over time. For example, which internal and external stakeholders, including subject matter experts, are important to consult and engage with? For example, does the business have a presence in the country in which their supplier is operating that enables them to carry out regular and reliable monitoring of environmental risks and/or effective systems for meaningful supplier and stakeholder engagement, where appropriate?
- **Establish RBC policy goals in compliance with domestic laws** and acknowledge the importance of applying the core principles of the mitigation hierarchy that prioritizes reducing or avoiding environmental impacts over restoration, compensation or offsetting measures when conducting risk management .[18] Enterprises may also seek to be responsive to gender equality issues linked to environmental protection.[19]
- **Seek to understand and address barriers arising from the enterprise's way of doing business that may impede the ability of suppliers to implement RBC policy expectations and/or contribute to adverse impacts in the supply chain** (such as the enterprise's purchasing practices, business and sourcing models and commercial incentives). Enterprises can also address the challenge of duplicative and conflicting supplier requirements through collaborating with other industry actors.
- **Embed expectations for suppliers** on the enterprise's most significant environmental risks. In addition to articulating expectations in RBC policies, enterprises can consider integrating due diligence expectations into pre-qualification processes, bidding criteria or screening criteria for new suppliers.

- **Defining specific policy red lines**. Enterprises may also choose to include detail on potential "red lines" in their RBC policies or in the expectations they set for new suppliers on environmental risks. Red lines may comprise situations that could –as a last resort –trigger disengagement from a supplier (e.g. where environmental risks or impacts are considered irremediable, where there is no reasonable prospect of change, or where severe impacts or risks are not immediately prevented or mitigated).

1.2 How can an enterprise ensure that its RBC policies are fit for purpose and progressively tailor them to the enterprise's most severe and likely risks?

Environmental policies and management systems may often focus on technical aspects without taking into account the views of relevant stakeholders and experts.[20] However, internal and external stakeholders and experts can play an important role in helping to ensure that RBC due diligence policy commitments are fit for purpose under OECD standards. Meaningful stakeholder engagement is a key component of the due diligence framework, although which stakeholders are relevant at a particular point in time and in a particular context will depend on the enterprise and its activities.[21]

Box 4. Meaningful stakeholder engagement

Meaningful stakeholder engagement is a key component of the due diligence process. In some cases, stakeholder engagement may also be a right in and of itself. Stakeholder engagement involves interactive processes of engagement with relevant stakeholders, through, for example, meetings, hearings or consultation proceedings. Relevant stakeholders are persons or groups, or their legitimate representatives, who have rights or interests related to the matters covered by the Guidelines that are or could be affected by adverse impacts associated with the enterprise's operations, products or services. Enterprises can prioritise the most severely impacted or potentially impacted stakeholders for engagement. The degree of impact on stakeholders may inform the degree of engagement. Meaningful stakeholder engagement refers to ongoing engagement with stakeholders that is two-way, conducted in good faith by the participants on both sides and responsive to stakeholders' views. To ensure stakeholder engagement is meaningful and effective, it is important to ensure that it is timely, accessible, appropriate and safe for stakeholders, and to identify and remove potential barriers to engaging with stakeholders in positions of vulnerability or marginalisation. The OECD Due Diligence Guidance for Responsible Business Conduct and relevant OECD sector specific guidance includes practical support for enterprises on carrying out stakeholder engagement including as part of an enterprise's due diligence process. This engagement is particularly important in the planning and decision-making concerning projects or other activities involving, for example, the intensive use of land or water, which could significantly affect local communities.

Source: Taken from the Commentary on Chapter II: General Policies of the OECD Guidelines for Multinational Enterprises on Responsible Business Conduct (OECD, 2023[16]), https://doi.org/10.1787/81f92357-en.

Stakeholder engagement in mineral supply chains will play a particularly important role in tailoring due diligence due to the way environmental impacts in mineral supply chains may affect people. Extractive industry activities can degrade soil quality and contribute to air and water pollution threatening resources upon which people depend for subsistence. Besides directly engaging with stakeholders in connection with an enterprise's operations, enterprises further downstream, as part of their own due diligence of supplier practices, could check to make sure stakeholder engagement takes place. When using stakeholder engagement as part of due diligence on environmental risks in mineral supply chains, enterprises should be aware of the nexus that often exists between environmental impacts and other RBC impacts addressed by the OECD Minerals Guidance like serious human rights abuses and corruption, with repression of environmental human rights defenders and different forms of corruption sometimes used to suppress community grievances or avoid accountability for environmental impacts.

When setting a policy on sourcing from small suppliers like ASM or associated small-scale processors, traders and smelters/refiners, attention should be paid to the limitations they may face in implementing corrective action plans in a timely and adequate manner. Consequently, policies still need to be set for small suppliers, but more flexibility should be allowed, with increasing stringency as the capacity of the supplier builds. For example, tailings management is important for ASM, but conformance with the Global Industry Standard on Tailings Management (GISTM) may not be appropriate because of the limited capacity of ASM suppliers and lower risks associated with smaller tonnages of tailings.[22]

Appropriate allocation of resources is critical for understanding to what extent an enterprise policy is fit for purpose. Following consultation and policy finalisation, a budget and resourcing system could be developed to support implementation, that could include:

- How the environmental and/or responsible sourcing management systems will be improved to support delivery on the policy's commitments,
- The parties responsible for policy implementation,
- How staff will be trained in the new policy and improved management systems,
- A communications and engagement plan defining how the policy will be communicated to customers and suppliers, and what and when new obligations will be included in new and existing contracts.

Finally, the monitoring of progress against RBC policy goals and specific targets and indicators under Step 4 helps enterprises to understand if its policies and management systems are addressing prioritised environmental risks and adverse impacts effectively. These type of feedback loops of lessons learned are important for continually improving processes and outcomes over time.

1.3 What is the relationship between existing environmental management systems (EMS) and environmental due diligence under OECD RBC standards?

Environmental management "involves carrying out risk-based due diligence with respect to adverse environmental impacts", in line with the MNE Guidelines. In the context of the Guidelines, the term "environmental management" is interpreted in a broad sense, embodying "activities aimed at understanding environmental impacts and risks, avoiding and addressing environmental impacts related to an enterprise's operations, products and services, taking into consideration the enterprise's share of cumulative impacts and continually seeking to improve an enterprise's environmental performance".

Improving environmental performance requires a commitment to a systematic approach and to continuous improvement. An EMS provides the internal framework necessary to integrate environmental considerations into business operations. Having such a system in place should help to assure shareholders, workers, employees and communities and other relevant stakeholders that the enterprise is actively working to protect the environment from the impact of its activities. Table 3 illustrates related elements of an EMS (based on ISO 14001:2015) and corresponding due diligence under the MNE Guidelines and RBC Guidance.

In practice, however, traditional environmental management systems may differ in scope and purpose from the expectations set out under the MNE Guidelines. For example, they may be focused only on environmental impacts associated with an enterprise's direct operations, rather than also taking into account risks and impacts across its supply chain and business relationships. They can entail a compliance-based approach against specific environmental targets rather than a risk-based approach aimed at continuous improvement over time, and they may not sufficiently provide for meaningful stakeholder engagement.

As such, enterprises can take into consideration existing environmental management systems as one tool to support their due diligence whilst addressing gaps that may exist in existing systems as compared to the risk-based due diligence process recommended by the MNE Guidelines. For downstream enterprises this may entail evaluating the scope and relevance of suppliers' environmental management systems and layering on their own due diligence.

Table 3. Integrating EMS into broader RBC considerations

Relevant step of the OECD Due Diligence Framework	Corresponding elements of an Environmental Management System (based on ISO 14001:2015)
Step 1: Embed RBC into policies and management systems	Ensuring leadership and commitment of an enterprise's top management, determining an environmental policy, organizational structures and processes for environmental management Ensuring necessary resources, competencies and adequate internal communication Understanding the context in which an enterprise operates, including the needs and expectations of its stakeholders and its legal requirements
Step 2: Identify and assess adverse impacts in operations, supply chains and business relationships	Identifying, assessing and internally communicating the environmental aspects and impacts and associated risks and opportunities Understanding the context in which an enterprise operates, including the needs and expectations of its stakeholders and its legal requirements
Step 3: Cease, prevent or mitigate adverse impacts	Establishing environmental objectives Planning and taking action
Step 4: Track implementation and results	Tracking implementation by evaluation of environmental performance and compliance Achieving continual improvement
Step 5: Communicate how impacts are addressed	Ensuring adequate external communication about the EMS and its outcomes
Step 6: Provide for or cooperate in remediation when appropriate and Step 3: Cease, prevent or mitigate adverse impacts	Address non-conformities and take corrective action.

Source: ISO 14001:2015 Environmental management systems – Requirements with guidance for use.

Step 2: Identify and assess actual and potential adverse impacts associated with enterprise operations, products or services

What does the RBC Guidance say?

- Carry out a **broad scoping exercise** to identify all areas of the business, across its operations and relationships, including in its supply chains, where RBC risks are most likely to be present and most significant.
- Starting with the significant areas of risk identified above, **map and carry out iterative and increasingly in-depth assessments** of prioritised operations, suppliers and other business relationships in order to identify and assess specific actual and potential adverse RBC impacts.
- **Assess the enterprise's involvement with the actual or potential adverse impacts** identified to determine the appropriate responses. Specifically, assess whether the enterprise: caused, contributed to or was directly linked to the impact by a business relationship (or would cause, contribute to or be directly linked to a potential impact).

- Drawing from the information obtained on actual and potential adverse impacts, where necessary, **prioritise the most significant RBC risks and impacts for action** based on severity and likelihood.

Key questions on how to integrate environmental risk considerations into this step:

- 2.1 What factors can an enterprise consider when **scoping and prioritising** environmental risks and impacts in its supply chain?
- 2.2 What types of information sources and tools can enterprises use to conduct **in-depth assessments** of prioritised suppliers on environmental risks and impacts?
- 2.3 What types of **indicators** may trigger enhanced due diligence?
- 2.4 What unique environmental risks and impacts can sourcing from **secondary sources** present?
- 2.5 When identifying and assessing **climate impacts**, what tools and resources are available for businesses to assess **GHG hotspots** in the supply chain?
- 2.6 How can an enterprise assess **ASM** involvement with actual or potential adverse environmental impacts?
- 2.7 How can an enterprise **evaluate its involvement** with identified environmental risks and adverse impacts in the supply chain?

2.1 What factors can an enterprise consider when scoping and prioritising environmental risks and impacts in its supply chain?

- Enterprises should carry out an initial high-level scoping exercise across their own operations and business relationships to identify and prioritise the most severe and likely environmental risk areas, taking into consideration sector, product, geographic and enterprise-level "risk factors".[23]
- Enterprises are expected to gather information from a range of sources for the purposes of the high-level scoping exercise, including information raised through early warning systems and grievance mechanisms and through engagement with relevant stakeholders and experts. The scoping should be updated with new information when the enterprise makes significant changes (e.g. operating in or sourcing from a new country; developing a new product or service line; engaging new forms of business relationship).

In the context of environmental impacts, some mining, smelting and refining processes have a greater environmental footprint than others and some geographies and biophysical environments are more sensitive than others. For example, businesses can consider the following factors:

Ecosystem type (terrestrial, marine and aquatic) and topography:

- Where operations are located in biodiverse areas, such as forests, wetlands or littoral zones, heightened due diligence must be undertaken in relation to the risk of adverse environmental impacts occurring. For example, an increasing number of exploration licenses in tropical and sub-tropical forests has been observed, and a growth of mines in forest landscapes and in countries with weak governance for managing mining/forests interactions is expected.
- While high biodiversity hotspots such as tropical forests deserve priority on the basis of biodiversity protection, in the context of mitigating climate impacts, the mining of peatlands, wetlands, grasslands and boreal forests is also highly destructive due to the carbon sequestration potential of the soils in these biomes, notwithstanding their own unique biodiversity.
- Areas where there are surface water and groundwater resources that support important aquatic ecosystems and/or human uses such as for drinking water and subsistence or other traditional uses are also areas to note. Mining operations can impact water quality and quantity and the

threshold for significant risks and impacts in areas of important aquatic and water resources may be lower than at other locations.

- Moreover, where operations are located in areas prone to heavy rainfall, the impacts of seismic activity on dams' integrity may be more consequential, with resulting increased risk for damage to physical operations (e.g. dam breaks resulting in uncontrolled acid and metalliferous drainage).

Type of mineral:

- Some mineral deposit types have intrinsically higher risk, due to high concentrations of radioactive minerals, reactive minerals, acid generating minerals, metal leaching minerals or toxic elements that can be more challenging to manage. Mining, processing, smelting and refining wastes from these types of operations can pose a higher risk to people and nature during the operating life and for long time periods following closure of operations.
- Increased risks are associated with the move to lower-grade ores, as they produce larger volumes of waste and require more energy, water and chemicals for processing.
- Different commodities produce different environmental impact specificities. Some metals have high specific impact (potentials), but only small impact in absolute terms due to lower volumes and mass flows, while other metals (iron/steel) show high overall impacts mostly because of their larger volumes and mass flows. More information can be found in the OECD's Global Material Resources Outlook to 2016 (OECD, 2019[17]).

Type of mining and processing:

- The techniques and chemicals used to process the raw material may determine the likelihood of environmental risks and adverse impact. In general, refining and smelting tend to require high amounts of energy, which in many cases come from fossil fuels, that generate GHG emissions. Transport and handling tend to produce large amounts of dust, volatile organic compounds and GHGs and generate noise emissions (Garbarino et al., 2021[18]). Mineral storage tends to raise issues around safety (structural, physical and chemical stability), can produce emissions to soil, water and air (to a lesser extent), and have an impact on habitats.
- Open pit mining may result in more land surface and air (dust) impacts than underground mining since the open pit land area and waste rock disposal areas take up more space as compared to underground mining. However, both underground and open pit mining can result in impacts to both water quality and quantity. Dewatering may be necessary during mine operations to keep mine workings dry and safe for miners, but this can impact water availability. Precipitation and runoff on and over mined surfaces and mining and processing wastes can result in mobilization of metals into adjacent lands, groundwater, and surface waters at both underground and open pit mines. Tailings impoundments can be a risk at many operations.

Identifying categories of materials, processes and ecosystems that may increase the severity and likelihood of environmental risks and impacts as part of an initial scoping exercise can provide indicators that inform a risk-based approach and enable the enterprise to carry out an initial prioritisation of the most significant risk areas for further assessment. Based on the prioritised risk issues, an enterprise can select individual higher-risk operations and business relationships for in-depth mapping and risk assessments to identify specific site-level risks and adverse impacts.

Moreover, risks and impacts can occur during and following mine closure. For example, some operations may have tailings dams and impoundments that must be monitored and maintained far into the future to ensure stability and prevent leakage, potential pollution and failures. Some operations require long-term water management and monitoring since runoff and seepage that contact mine waste, tailings, pit and underground mine walls can remain a risk and potential source of impacts long after the mine closes. Post-closure environmental impacts can be as or more significant than risks during the mining operation itself if closure activities have not been implemented properly. In addition, there might be a higher probability that mitigation measures are not maintained or fail if the mining operator is no longer actively at the site and generating income to fund post-closure monitoring and maintenance.

2.2 What types of information sources and tools can enterprises use to conduct in-depth assessments of prioritised suppliers on environmental risks and impacts?

- Enterprises are expected to carry out proportionate and risk-based assessments of prioritised suppliers to identify and assess specific environmental impacts. For most types of risks, assessments will broadly cover:
  - Actual or potential adverse impacts caused or contributed to by the supplier, including those associated with future projects or activities
  - The capacity and willingness of suppliers to carry out due diligence
  - The adequacy of the due diligence carried out, including measures to prevent, mitigate and remediate relevant environmental risks and impacts (Steps 3 and 6).
- Seek to collect sufficient information to assess the nature and extent of actual and potential impacts linked to prioritised suppliers and identify information gaps or blind spots. They have a range of tools and sources of information at their disposal to evaluate different types of environmental risks and impacts (see Table 4).
- The type of assessment and information sources that are appropriate in a specific context will depend, among other things, on the nature of the environmental risk, its severity and likelihood, where in the supply chain the risk is situated, and the position in the supply chain of each entity with a relationship to the risk or impact.

For example, where risks are situated in the furthest upstream segments of the supply chain, at or close to the point of extraction, downstream enterprises should obtain, when appropriate and feasible, information about business relationships beyond contractual suppliers and establish processes to assess the risk profile of more remote tiers of the supply chain. This can be done individually or collaboratively and can include reviewing existing supplier audits or other assessments, engaging with relevant mid-stream actors and/or control points (such as smelters, refiners and international concentrate traders) in the supply chain to assess the quality of their due diligence (see Figure 1), and consulting with relevant stakeholders.

The emphasis for downstream enterprises' risk assessments in such a situation will generally be on assessing and improving the due diligence management systems of control points who tend to have greater visibility and leverage over other upstream segments. Alternatively, if a risk or adverse impact is situated at the control point itself, downstream enterprises' risk assessments may focus on the control points' own mitigation, prevention and remediation activities.

Table 4. Examples of indicators and sources of information for identifying and assessing key environmental risks in upstream supply chains lists some examples of generic sources of information for evaluating environmental risk or impact categories against possible indicators; Annex B provides more detail with examples of the types of organisations, tools and online resources.

Table 4. Examples of indicators and sources of information for identifying and assessing key environmental risks in upstream supply chains

Environmental issues	Potential data and Indicators	Non exhaustive list of potential sources of information and helpful tools
Biodiversity loss (e.g. deforestation, coral reef degradation, species	Area taken up by operations Species at risk	EMS Environmental and social impact assessments (ESIAs), including biodiversity management plans, biodiversity

Environmental issues	Potential data and Indicators	Non exhaustive list of potential sources of information and helpful tools
loss) and damage to protected areas	Measures of ecosystem health using biomonitoring data Ecosystem services impacted Proximity to key biodiversity areas Destroyed area of valuable habitats Disturbance of wildlife Area deforested % of key biodiversity areas that may be impacted by operations Information on physical hazards and toxicity from materials to human health and the environment during the handling, transport and use of these materials.	action plans, mine closure plans and biodiversity offset plans Academic, industry and non-governmental organisation (NGO) studies Ongoing monitoring data from government or the supplier Environmental and water management programme reports from government or the supplier National / regional guidelines and assessments on biodiversity assets and natural capital Earth observation tools and software International bodies such as the Convention on Biological Diversity (CBD) may have additional data available for certain regions.
Climate change (e.g. GHG emissions , failure to adapt to physical risks of climate change)	Scope 1, 2 and 3 GHG emissions Alignment with relevant targets and transition pathways	The entity's net-zero transition plan The entity's climate change adaptation plan Sources of information related to the credibility of net-zero transition plans including e.g. Race to Zero Criteria, UNHLEG Integrity Matters report EMS ESIAs Environmental and Social Management Programmes (ESMPs) Life Cycle Assessments (LCAs) GHG reporting frameworks Academic, industry and NGO studies and expert engagement Compliance with GHG emission standards Carbon Disclosure Project data
Improper use and disposal of hazardous materials	Amount and types of hazardous materials used Quantity of hazardous materials released into air or water sources Information on physical hazards and toxicity from materials to human health and the environment during the handling, transport and use of these materials	EMS ESIAs ESMPs LCAs Academic, industry and NGO studies Safety Data Sheets
Noise and vibration	Intensity and frequency of noise generated Intensity and frequency of vibrations	ESIAs EMS ESMPs Community monitoring systems Academic, industry and NGO studies
Physical instability, soil erosion and land degradation	Number and frequency of tailings storage facility breaches Number and frequency of slope failures Volume of potentially unstable material Earthquake risk Data on soil quality	Feasibility stabilities Geotechnical studies Slope monitoring data Earthquake risk assessment Earthquake monitoring data EMS ESIAs ESMPs Geotechnical studies Participatory stakeholder monitoring
Pollution (air, water etc)	Air emissions (excluding GHGs) – amount and types Type and quantity of pollutants discharged Number of people living in the local area (watershed, airshed) Number of people dependent on local freshwater for domestic use	EMS ESIAs ESMPs LCAs Central and regional government monitoring networks Academic, industry and NGO studies Safety Data Sheets Census information for the local area

Environmental issues	Potential data and Indicators	Non exhaustive list of potential sources of information and helpful tools
	Number of people dependent on local environment (e.g. rivers, lakes, forests and biodiversity) for food security and nutrition Number or people afflicted with pollution related illnesses Information on physical hazards and toxicity from materials to human health and the environment during the handling, transport and use of these materials.	Socioeconomic and ecosystem services baseline studies Participatory stakeholder monitoring
Damage to aesthetics and cultural heritage sites	Area taken up by operations Number of complaints about impacts on cultural heritage sites or visual aesthetics	ESIAs ESMPs Academic, industry and NGO studies
Waste mismanagement	Waste generated (amount and type) Waste management system % of tailings with liners in place to minimise seepage Type of seepage management design implemented % of tailings storage facilities with closure cover % of waste rock dumps with closure covers, where required Information on physical hazards and toxicity from materials to human health and the environment during the handling, transport and use of these materials.	EMS ESIAs ESMPs LCAs Academic, industry and NGO studies Safety Data Sheets
Water depletion	Water use Data on water scarcity Water shed balance incl. other uses Surface water streamflow Groundwater level Proximity to other mines Water shed balances Water Footprint (ISO 14046)	Hydrology studies and models EMS ESIAs conducted in the area, ESMPs Academic, industry and NGO studies Community monitoring systems LCAs Reports on water depletion, impacts on water availability for users

Note: This table corresponds to the table on environmental risks in Chapter 2 of this Handbook.

Other sources and types of information that enterprises may find relevant when evaluating environmental risks associated with suppliers include:

- **Details of relevant supplier's RBC policies, business and sourcing models** with specific regard to prioritised environmental risk issues
- **Details of existing EMS,** including whether they have been verified by an independent third party.
- **Details of existing ESIAs**, including whether undertaken by an independent party and the extent of engagement with local communities during research, drafting and finalisation, and other environmental assessments, permits authorisations and permissions (see Box 4).
- **Early warning systems established by suppliers,** to identify and prevent environmental impacts. These include four key elements: risk knowledge, monitoring and warning system, communication and dissemination of warnings, and supplier response capability (UNISDR, 2008[19]).
- **Details on suppliers' strategies to address environmental impacts**, for example, improvements in efficiency (use of appropriate equipment, process optimizations, etc.), renewable energy deployment (on-site energy storage, electrification of vehicle fleet, etc.), energy intensity reduction and neutralization.
- **Locations of relevant operations and concession areas**, including exposure to extreme natural events, water stress, proximity to sensitive areas such as water sources, protected areas and other high value biodiversity areas and natural resources and human settlements. World Resources

Institute's (WRI) Aqueduct Water Risk Atlas (World Resources Institute, 2021[20]) as well as Integrated Biodiversity Assessment Tool Alliance tools (IBAT Alliance, n.d.[21]) are available to determine water stress and biodiversity risk.

- **Information on land clearance** and restoration (as % of total asset / concession land size) including deforestation and reforestation (as % of total asset / concession land size).
- **Closure plans**, covering decommissioning, social closure plans and site rehabilitation and financial provisions for this purpose.

Box 5. Environmental and Social Impact Assessments (ESIAs)

In most jurisdictions a supplier whose activities give rise to significant risks and impacts (such as a mining operator) will be required to conduct an ESIA. ESIAs generally take into consideration the sensitivity, quality, and values associated with the biophysical, cultural and social environment should a risk occur, and the capacity of the receiving environment and populations to cope with resulting impacts. It should also consider the extent (geographic extent/distance, magnitude, intensity, duration) and likely consequence of impacts arising from the risk (IAIA, n.d.[22])

In addition to be being part of due diligence, the content of an ESIA can be a source of information used in due diligence processes. However, the specific content will vary from one jurisdiction to another and depend on the nature of the proposed operation being assessed. The quality and credibility of the ESIA can vary according to, for example independence of the assessor or expert team, credibility, rigor and depth of information provided, level and quality of stakeholder engagement, and level of transparency, among other factors. Where doubts arise about the quality or independence of an ESIA, the enterprise should not rely on information in the ESIA for its due diligence process.

Downstream enterprises can furthermore consider gathering information for example through:

- **Information raised through supply chain grievance mechanisms** and other monitoring platforms, including to evaluate the effectiveness of operational level grievance-mechanisms.
- **Meaningful engagement with relevant stakeholders and/or experts**, including stakeholders affected (or potentially affected) by adverse environmental impacts associated with the enterprise's operations, products or services, or their legitimate representatives.
- **On-site inspections or assessments**, where possible, at prioritised suppliers (including with a local expert to build an understanding of the supplier, its activities and production and due diligence processes).[24]
- **Existing assessments** of prioritised suppliers, for example by multi-stakeholder, industry or government-run initiatives ("sustainability initiatives"') (such as ISO14001 audits or assessments by the Copper Mark, Initiative for Responsible Mining Assurance (IRMA), Towards Sustainable Mining (TSM), Responsible Jewellery Council (RJC), International Council on Mining and Metals (ICMM), World Gold Council (WGC), Responsible Steel, Aluminium Stewardship Initiative (ASI), the International Tin Association's Tin Code), and the Environmental Social Guidance Standard for Mineral Supply Chains of the Responsible Minerals Initiative/Responsible Business Alliance.
- **Other collaborative approaches with industry actors**, for example in sensitive landscapes that host significant production of a specific mineral category, enterprises can cooperate and jointly finance a Strategic Environmental Assessment at the level of the landscape (to be defined by relevant stakeholders) as opposed to specific operations (European Union, 2021[23]), to achieve economies of scale, identify cumulative impacts and priority issues to inform their sourcing strategies, and cooperate in reducing the severity or likelihood of certain risks arising (see Box 3 for an example of collaborative approaches to assessing environmental risks). This could be done

for example through an industry platform or multistakeholder initiative such as the Responsible Mineral Initiative (industry-led) or the European Partnership for Responsible Minerals and the Public Private Alliance for Responsible Minerals (multi-stakeholder).

- **Supplier reporting and disclosures**, for example, sustainability reports, climate and biodiversity disclosures (See Annex B) or in industry benchmarking initiatives such as those established by third-parties, as well as credible public reports. Earth observation tools or other geospatial data providers can be used to monitor observable changes in the landscape around a supplier's operations, if relevant.[25]
- **Checking for issues prevalent in the region or area** where a supply chain actor operates (for example, if a supplier operates in a region where several spillages have taken place as a result of shipping incidents, which caused damage to marine ecosystems, and the integrity of local transport and logistics within the supply chain can be checked).

Importantly, enterprises retain ultimate responsibility for their own due diligence under international standards. If using findings or other information from an industry, government-run or multi-stakeholder initiative to support their due diligence, enterprises should review the information to ensure that it is credible, relevant and up-to-date.[26]

Information blind spots

Enterprises, particularly those at greater remove or separated by several tiers in the supply chain from where the risk or adverse impact is situated, will naturally identify areas where they lack information or independent data to assess environmental risks. In some cases, it may not be possible to gather the necessary information and in others, an enterprise may not have the right expertise to know which questions to ask or where to look. Another example of blind spots is information on issues that have not yet manifested, for example, environmental impacts that may take place after a mine or smelting plant closure.

In these cases and depending on context, engagement with joint buyers or other relevant suppliers, intermediaries and stakeholders can be particularly important (e.g. relevant local NGOs, workers or their representatives or other impacted or potentially impacted stakeholders). For example, engagement with traders is important for gathering information on risks associated with transport and logistics activities, which often receive limited attention and where environmental impacts can be significant. Efforts to increase leverage over relevant suppliers or control points can also be important where enterprises lack necessary information (see discussion on Step 3 below).

2.3 What types of conditions may trigger enhanced due diligence?

Indicators of potentially high risk can be relevant to the risk scoping and assessment process under Step 2 and trigger enhanced due diligence efforts. Table 5 sets out illustrative, non-exhaustive examples of conditions related to mining, processing, smelting, recycling or refining activities which enterprises may warrant enhanced due diligence, depending on the context and the outcomes of their Step 2 scoping exercise.

Table 5. Illustrative examples of conditions related to mining, processing, smelting, recycling or refining activities (according to risk type) that may warrant enhanced due diligence

Type of environmental risk	Illustrative examples of conditions that may warrant enhanced due diligence
Biodiversity loss (e.g. deforestation, coral reef degradation, species loss)	• Operation in or close to World Heritage Sites. • Operation in or close to sensitive, highly valued, protected locations, such as areas of High Conservation Value, biodiversity hot spots, International Union for Conservation of Nature (IUCN) Protected Areas

Type of environmental risk	Illustrative examples of conditions that may warrant enhanced due diligence
and damage to protected areas	categories I-IV, Ramsar sites, primary rainforest, United Nations Educational, Scientific and Cultural Organization (UNESCO) Biosphere Reserves, and other effective area-based conservation units. • Operation in or close to critical habitat as defined by International Finance Corporation (IFC) Performance Standard 6 (PS6). • Losses of significant biodiversity within the direct and indirect footprint of the activities (as defined by IFC Performance Standards 1 (PS1) and 6 (PS6). • Deforestation or mining activities in forested areas. • Deep-sea or marine mining that is unregulated by the International Seabed Authority or relevant national authorities, or where credible studies demonstrate irreversible damage to the marine environment may or will occur within and/or beyond the mining boundary.
Climate change (e.g. GHG emissions , failure to adapt to physical risks of climate change)	• Operation damaging carbon sinks such as high carbon stock forests or peatlands. • Operation relies solely/heavily on fossil fuels for its energy needs. • Operation failing to establish and implement a decarbonisation plan and adopt, implement, monitor and report on short, medium and long-term mitigation targets aligned with internationally agreed global temperature goals. • Operation leading to lock-in of carbon intensive assets. • Operation failing to establish and implement a climate change adaptation plan to prepare and respond to current and future climate change impacts.
Improper use and disposal of hazardous materials	• Operation using mercury in the recovery of gold. • Operation is using cyanide in the recovery of gold outside of the recognised management regime of the International Cyanide Management Code. • Inappropriate recycling and processing of used lead-acid batteries and other lead scrap that results in environmental damage.
Noise and vibration	• Wildlife migrating from an area near a mine site due to noise. • Local communities being severely impacted by noise.
Physical instability, soil erosion and land degradation	• Open pit slope and waste rock dump failure. • Rock bursts, subsidence and sinkhole development. • Tailings storage facility failure. • Slag dump failure. • Loss of soil as a resource through erosion and degradation of soil quality.
Pollution (air, water, soil)	• Operation has resulted in pollution requiring treatment in perpetuity. • Emissions from smelting and refining are not captured and treated. • Acid metalliferous drainage or the discharge of warm cooling water from smelter operations causing rapid thermal changes in the receiving environment. • Uncontrolled releases of sediments and process chemicals, such as mercury from artisanal mine workings, into surface or ground waters. • Emissions of sulphur dioxide from roasting sulphide concentrates in base metal smelters, fluoride from aluminium smelters, polychlorinated dibenzodioxins especially from copper or iron ore sinter plants or arsenic, lead, cadmium and mercury from smelters that are associated with adverse impacts on land and soil quality and ecosystem and human health. • Dioxins and furans from open burning of plastic-coated metal-containing products, such as building wire. • Soil contamination near mining, refining and smelting from emissions deposition or waste disposal.
Destruction of cultural heritage sites and damage to aesthetics	• Operation will irreversibly damage or degrade cultural or sacred heritage sites, including World Heritage Sites. • Operation that may temporarily cause adverse impacts on sacred sites or constrain access to such sites. • Operation has impaired local community's ability to enjoy and benefit from their environment.
Waste mismanagement	• Mining, mineral processing, smelting and refining generating large amounts of hazardous and non-hazardous waste that is not safely disposed of (as well as marketable by-products such as slags). For example, operation is disposing tailings into river, lake or coastal waters.
Water depletion	• Operations takes place within arid and water scarce regions. • Operations that may deteriorate water quality, degrade or constrain access to natural resources, particularly those used by Indigenous Peoples or local communities. • Reduced access to clean water for local communities. • Credible and independent studies demonstrate water consumption is unsustainable regarding quality or quantity or limiting access to adequate water for other water users. • Rerouting of surface waters to generate hydropower in remote locations where grid electricity is not available, resulting in reduced access to clean water for local communities.

Type of environmental risk	Illustrative examples of conditions that may warrant enhanced due diligence
Other	• Operator does not have a closure and reclamation plan for its facilities (mainly relevant to mines), with financial guarantees or the plan is out of date relative to current activities. • Persistent and egregious non-compliance with national laws and regulations related to environmental management and performance outcomes (reputation as a serial polluter). • Indication of corruption related to environmental management and performance outcomes. • Ongoing or unresolved serious human rights violations (including those mediated through environmental impacts) related to the supplier's business activities, including against Indigenous Peoples and environmental and human rights defenders. • Lack of, or poor quality / poorly accessible, disclosure on environmental incidents and impacts. • Evidence of Greenwashing by the operator. • No disclosure of environmental impact assessment findings and recommendations. • Potential impacts on Indigenous Peoples. • Lack of meaningful engagement with communities. • Lack of consent from Indigenous Peoples or communities for involuntary resettlement from their traditional lands and natural resources.

1. Enterprises operating at the boundaries of protected locations, or that have protected areas within their zone of influence, can have huge impacts on protected areas, and thus may also warrant enhanced due diligence.
2. See Annex II of the OECD Due Diligence Guidance for Responsible Supply Chains of Minerals from Conflict-Affected and High-Risk Areas (OECD, 2016[24]) for more detailed information on serious human rights abuses.

2.4 What unique environmental risks and impacts can sourcing secondary sources present?

While they offer the opportunity to avoid environmental harms linked to mining and mineral processing, secondary materials are not free of risks and adverse impacts and present unique challenges when conducting supply chain due diligence. For example, adverse impacts on people and nature have been documented for lead acid battery recycling (Lead Recycling Africa Project, 2016[25]) and electronics recycling (UNEP, 2022[26]; UNEP, n.d.[27]).

Risks associated with poorly managed recycling include:

- Contamination of air, soil and water, related human health impacts and bioaccumulation of heavy metals in food chains.
- Exposure of workers to hazardous materials and related health impacts.
- Incomplete recovery and removal of hazardous substances during recycling, leading to contamination of products made from the recycled feedstock.
- Additional land usage and occupation by (informal) landfills for remnants of incomplete recycled initial products.

Special care is necessary when sourcing secondary materials from opaque supply chains i.e. when the source of the secondary material is uncertain. For some metals, such as gold, if the recycled metal is not subjected to due diligence, it can enable the laundering of materials mined in a harmful and illicit manner, including those contributing to serious environmental issues, as well as conflict and human rights violations. Enterprises sourcing recycled metal can, as a first step, verify the material is indeed recycled, and not partially processed mined material being passed off as recycled.

The next step is to understand the risk profile of different minerals (e.g. what chemicals are used for extraction, what emissions are caused through the recycling process, are they commonly processed together with other materials that may cause environmental damage). As part of a risk-based approach, enterprises may also need to determine where the recycling takes place, as location can significantly influence risks. Enterprises should complete a broad risk assessment of the recycler's sources of supply, identify any conditions that may warrant enhanced due diligence if/where necessary. In many cases the adverse impacts of secondary materials might be blind-spots, and enterprises might need to tailor their due diligence approach to identify those blind-spots and consider how to tackle them (see answer to question 2.2 on types of information sources and tools can enterprises use to conduct in-depth assessments of prioritised suppliers on environmental risks and impacts?).

2.5 When identifying and assessing climate impacts, what tools and resources are available for businesses to assess GHG hotspots in the supply chain?

Risk-based identification and assessment of emissions is the first and most crucial step towards emission reduction target setting and GHG mitigation. The GHG Protocol classifies an enterprise's emissions into three scopes:

- 'Scope 1' – direct GHG emissions that are from sources owned or controlled by the reporting entity, such as those emissions from the production and transportation equipment owned by the entity.
- 'Scope 2' – indirect GHG emissions associated with the production of electricity, heat, or steam purchased by the reporting entity.
- 'Scope 3' – all other indirect emissions (for example, associated with the production of purchased materials, fuels, and services, including transport in vehicles not owned or controlled by the reporting entity, outsourced activities).

Enterprises should assess their Scope 1, 2 and, to the extent possible based on best available information, scope 3 GHG emissions in order to identify where their most severe and likely impacts lie. Upstream enterprise emissions primarily fall under Scope 3 and in many cases, the crushing of ore as well as the chemical processing stage of mineral supply chains (i.e. refining and smelting) is a hotspot for GHG emissions based on their sources of energy and chemicals usage. It is important to assess emissions against the latest available scientific evidence and as different national or industry specific transition pathways are developed and updated. It is crucial to collect information on emissions from upstream suppliers so this can be integrated into the Scope 3 assessment.

Useful frameworks for corporate GHG accounting are the GHG Protocol, Responsible Steel GHG Standard, and the EU Environmental Footprint Method. Other useful frameworks to identify the carbon footprint of products (rather than of an enterprise) include the Global Battery Alliance's Battery Passport GHG Rulebook (under development), the International Zinc Association Carbon Footprint Guidance for Zinc Production (under development), RE100 Technical Criteria, GHG Protocol Scope 2 Guidance and ISO 14040, 14044, and 14067.

2.6 How to assess ASM involvement with actual or potential adverse environmental impacts?

When sourcing from ASM, the following questions may provide a useful framework for approaching environmental risk assessments on prioritised environmental issues. To answer the following questions, an enterprise may wish to work in collaboration with other actors who are also sourcing directly or indirectly from the region. As mentioned at the top of this Chapter, the relevance of these questions will vary according to the enterprise's position in the supply chain and its involvement with the risk in question. See also Figure 1.

General risk profile:

- What is ASM mining? How does production work? Is any part of the process mechanised?
- How risk-aware are the owners, leaders, workers? How and how well are the miners already controlling risk? What incentives exist already for them to manage and minimise risk? What are

the barriers to controlling risk (generally and specifically environmental risks)? What would need to change to improve that?

- Is the organisation part of any sustainable development, government or community programme to tackle environmental or human rights issues, or supported by any local support organisations?
- What would happen to the miners and their families if they could not mine or sell their product into formal supply chains? What else could/would they do and what would be the impact of those activities?

Environmental impacts:

- Where is the mining happening? What is the ecological sensitivity of this location? What is its conservation status?
- How is the mining and any processing done and how is waste managed? Are explosives, fuel and chemicals used?
- Is there a Safety Data Sheet for the material?[27] Is the Safety Data Sheet up to date (not older than 5 years)?
- Where and how do miners live while they are mining? Consider impacts of housing, subsistence, transportation between home and mine, for example miners' reliance on wild meat or bush meat for protein, timbering for struts and tools etc.
- How does the miners' presence stimulate others to act in ways that impact on the ecosystem? Economic stimulus through raising awareness of or access to previously remote places, for example agriculturalists, hunters, lumberjacks use footpaths to penetrate wilderness and exploit natural resources, etc.
- How is the material transported to customers? Are there any organisms or environments (receptors) that could be negatively affected by the material or its transportation?

Where environmental impacts are cumulative in nature:

- Is there a bioaccumulation risk[28] or a chronic toxicity effect[29] indicated on the Safety Data Sheet for the material?
- How many other ASM organisations operate in the area?
- What is the overall ASM population in the area?
- If possible to determine over time, what capacity does your supplier have to meet due diligence expectations (for example, in terms of organisational competence, environmental awareness, nature of adverse impacts, quality of risk management)?
- What other economic activities exist that may extend, deepen or magnify your supplier's direct and indirect impacts?
- What relationships exist between your supplier and these other actors that could be leveraged to organise a more landscape level approach to risk management?[30] What relationships exist between you and other stakeholders to explore collective leverage to tackle issues at the landscape level?

Mine closure and post-mining: [31]

- What are the legal requirements and to what extent are these enforced?
- What plan – if any – is in place to avoid damage to the land as a result of post-closure ASM? What approach is being used or will be used to rehabilitate or restore lands degraded by ASM? Who holds responsibility for this and how realistic is it that closure will be done at all or well? Is this approach economically affordable, socially acceptable and ecologically viable?

- Who holds responsibilities in active mine closure? And in post-closure monitoring and maintenance? How are miners, landowners, communities and local authorities involved in closure and post-mining phases?
- What is the planned end purpose for the closed land (for example forestry, agriculture, natural forest, etc.)? How does this account for economic, social and environmental sustainability, including contributions to helping nature thrive either directly or indirectly?

Step 3: Cease, prevent, and mitigate adverse impacts

What does the RBC Guidance say?

- Stop (cease) activities that are causing or contributing to adverse environmental impacts.
- Develop and implement plans to prevent or mitigate actual or potential adverse environmental impacts.
- Appropriate responses to risks and impacts associated with business relationships can include:
  - build and use leverage, to the extent possible, to prompt the business relationship(s) to prevent or mitigate adverse impacts or risks;
  - continuation of the relationship throughout the course of risk mitigation efforts;
  - temporary suspension of the relationship while pursuing ongoing risk mitigation; or
  - disengagement with the business relationship either after failed attempts at preventing or mitigating severe impacts, when adverse impacts are irremediable, where there is no reasonable prospect of change, or when severe impacts or risks are identified and the entity causing the impact does not take immediate action to prevent or mitigate. Critically, **disengagement is a measure of last resort.** A decision to disengage should consider the potential adverse social and economic impacts of disengaging and be done responsibly.[32]

What additional mineral-specific recommendations are in the Minerals Guidance?

- FOR UPSTREAM: Identify and track which suppliers respond to information requests and which do not. Follow up with suppliers and set corrective action plans. Escalate uncooperative suppliers to senior management.
- FOR DOWNSTREAM: If the point of transformation for the mineral cannot be identified, adopt a risk management plan to be able to eventually demonstrate significant measurable improvements to your efforts to do so. If the point of transformation can be identified, work with suppliers to establish measurable risk-mitigation actions intended to promote progressive performance improvement within a reasonable timescale.

Key questions on how to integrate environmental risk considerations into this step:

- 3.1 How can an enterprise evaluate its involvement with identified environmental risks and adverse impacts in the supply chain?
- 3.2 What actions can enterprises take to address identified harms in the supply chain? How can enterprises use their leverage?
- 3.3 What types of prevention and mitigation measures can enterprises reasonably expect of suppliers that are causing or contributing to significant environmental impacts?
- 3.4 How does the interaction between environment and human rights affect enterprise action to cease, prevent, and mitigate adverse environmental impacts?

3.1 How can an enterprise evaluate its involvement with identified environmental risks and adverse impacts in the supply chain?

An entity's involvement or relationship to impacts in the supply chain is important because it establishes where the primary responsibility for addressing the impact lies, and how the enterprise is expected to respond (see Figure 4). An enterprise's relationship to adverse impacts is not static. It may change, for example as situations evolve and depending on the degree to which due diligence and steps taken to address identified risks and impacts decrease the risk of the impacts occurring. See discussion of Step 3 below.

Figure 4. Addressing adverse impacts

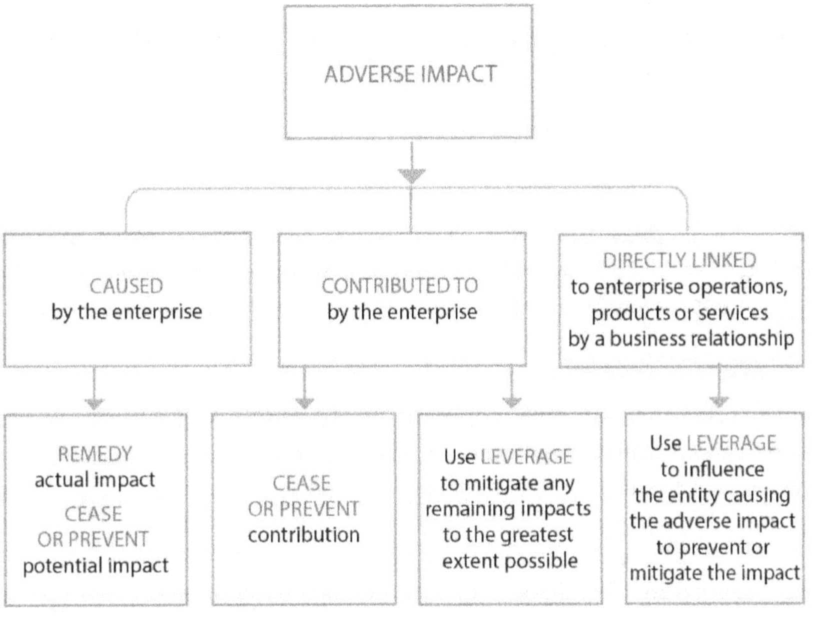

Source: OECD (2018[15]), *OECD Due Diligence Guidance for Responsible Business Conduct*, https://mneguidelines.oecd.org/OECD-Due-Diligence-Guidance-for-Responsible-Business-Conduct.pdf.

An enterprise "*causes*" an adverse environmental impact if its activities on their own are sufficient to result in the adverse impact. An enterprise "*contributes to*" an adverse environmental impact if its activities, in combination with the activities of other entities cause the impact, or if the activities of the enterprise cause, facilitate or incentivise another entity to cause an adverse impact. Adverse environmental impacts can also be *directly linked* to an enterprise's business operations, products or services by a business relationship, even if they do not contribute to those impacts.

3.2 What actions can enterprises take to address identified harms in the supply chain? How can enterprises use their leverage?

The risk-based due diligence approach is again integral to implementing Step 3. As it will often not be possible for enterprises to identify or respond to all identified risks and adverse impacts associated with their suppliers simultaneously, enterprises can prioritise specific risks and impacts for action on the basis of severity[33] and likelihood. They should move on to address less severe impacts once prioritised impacts have been addressed. The same principles apply to how their suppliers should in turn prioritise risks and impacts for action.

As mentioned in Step 2, the enterprise's relationship to an identified risk or impact determines the responsibility it has for addressing the impact. For example, where enterprises identify that they are causing or contributing to (or may cause or contribute to) environmental risks or impacts, they face heightened responsibilities, including to cease the activity contributing to harm and to provide remediation under Step 6 (see Figure 4). They are also expected to adopt prevention and mitigation measures, *including through using and building leverage* over other entities causing harm. Where enterprises identify that they are directly linked to an impact, they are expected to seek to prevent and mitigate impacts, including *through using and building leverage* (see also "What does the RBC Guidance say", above).

Using leverage of suppliers is broadly understood and captures incentivising, supporting and otherwise effecting change in the behaviour of a business relationship (or other entity causing harm). How an enterprise chooses to support, incentivise or otherwise apply leverage over an individual business relationship will depend on the context –including the nature of its relationship, the degree of leverage it has, the nature of the risk or impact, and the supplier's capacity to prevent, mitigate or remediate the impact.

Enterprises can consider adapting purchasing practices and business models or using leverage over their suppliers in a number of ways, for example by:

- **Using enterprise policies or codes of conduct, contracts, written agreements or market power**. Building expectations around RBC and due diligence specifically into commercial contracts and linking business incentives – such as the commitment to long-term contracts and future orders – with performance on RBC. Clearly communicating the consequences if expectations around RBC are not respected (e.g. through meeting with management of the business relationship).
- **Supporting or collaborating with suppliers in developing fit-for-purpose plans** for them to prevent or mitigate adverse environmental impacts (for example, net zero transition plans). In instances where suppliers may require guidance, capacity building or support on how to manage risks and prevent impacts occurring and address barriers or challenges, enterprises may support suppliers in reviewing the environmental risk controls in place, identifying gaps, and putting in place a corrective action plan. Suppliers may also require support and guidance on how to identify whether or not harm has occurred or may be imminent.
- **Supporting suppliers in the prevention or mitigation of adverse impacts or risks**, e.g. through training, upgrading of facilities, or strengthening of their management systems: When sourcing from ASM, enterprises can work in partnership with the ASM cooperative or a specialist NGO that facilitates ASM cooperation, community representatives, local government, or multi-stakeholder ASM initiatives to support the ASM entity better manage its environmental corrective action plans. A helpful resource for ASM formalisation is the Code of Risk-mitigation for artisanal and small-scale mining engaging in Formal Trade (CRAFT Code), which is an open source tool for ASM and businesses potentially sourcing from the sector that sets progressive requirements for ASM. Ensuring that prevention and mitigation activities are appropriate requires collaboration with local stakeholders. To support the more systemic prevention and mitigation of environmental impacts over the long term, enterprises in the supply chain can play an important role in supporting the empowerment of local environmental NGOs and civil society organisations that work in collaboration with government and business, as well as local enforcement authorities.
- **Redesigning products to enable the substitution of materials or the use of secondary materials.** Some minerals are substitutable within a product. Downstream enterprises may wish to make product design decisions based upon the relative environmental performance across candidate materials, such as the relative carbon footprint, water footprint, dependency on mining in forests or sensitive ecosystems, the toxicity of wastes and the efficiency of production. A full

lifecycle analysis (cradle to grave) can support enterprises when making material substitution decisions, which can affect environmental performance of the product in its use and end-of-life phases.

- **Supply chain and public-private partnerships** are one way large and small enterprises can work together to generate leverage, pool resources and conduct more efficient due diligence, especially when they do this visibly and with the ambition of leading the sector. For example, the Dutch Metals Agreement uses individual risk assessments of businesses to produce a collective heat-map showing industry risks (SER, n.d.[28]). These individual business risk assessments are submitted to the Secretariat of the Agreement which aggregates and anonymizes information to produce the heat map.
- **Other types of multi-stakeholder, industry-led and government-run initiatives** can be a tool for enhancing collaboration across diverse industry players and their stakeholders, including by making joint statements to raise awareness about specific environmental concerns. Using a collective voice can also be helpful in co-creating solutions that can make environmental due diligence more feasible, more effective and thus more likely. There are also many industry initiatives that aim to develop global programs to assess, audit and improve sustainability practices within the industry's supply chains.

There may be considerable variability in the capacity of enterprises to apply their leverage over suppliers and, in turn, the capacity of their suppliers to use their leverage over their sub-suppliers. Where an enterprise lacks leverage, it is expected to increase its leverage where possible, for example through modifying commercial incentives, engaging with industry peers, establishing longer-term relationships with suppliers or participating in collaborative industry, multi-stakeholder or government-run initiatives.

When sourcing from large refiners, smelters, recyclers or miners, downstream enterprises and control points like smelters or refiners may pay particular attention to the capacities, influence and resources the supplier may have to implement corrective actions and use their market leverage accordingly. Understanding if the supplier is participating in or assessed by industry or multi-stakeholder initiatives, for example, can orient the buyer on what influence may be exerted on the one hand (loss of market access through membership status) and what other resources or support may be available through the association (member services). As well as setting standards for enterprises, many initiatives offer tools, training or peer-to-peer learning opportunities for members and suppliers on specific challenges.

Box 6. Understanding and complying with a growing body of legislation that supports the Rights of Nature

Ecosystem services[34] tend to be more protected by law than the intrinsic values of nature that are independent of human uses. However, jurisdictions are increasingly protecting the value of nature through 'rights for nature' laws (UN, 2022[29]) and a growing number of national and subnational governments and their courts have recognised legal personality of nature in recent years.

If a supplier is sourcing from a jurisdiction which acknowledges the rights of nature, work with the supplier to identify what additional risk management processes they have had to adopt to fulfil their responsibilities in this regard. If a supplier is not sourcing from a provenance that has afforded rights to nature, determine whether it would align with your business' values to encourage suppliers to introduce measures that go beyond the consideration of how harm to the environment may manifest as harm to people, but also to nature.

3.2 What types of prevention and mitigation measures can enterprises reasonably expect of suppliers that are causing or contributing to significant environmental impacts?

The prevention and mitigation measures that are appropriate and proportionate in a particular situation will depend on a range of factors, including the nature, severity and likelihood of the environmental issue in question, the supplier's involvement with the impact and, where it is contributing to an impact, the degree of leverage it has over other suppliers or entities causing harm. Table 6 provides examples of possible prevention and mitigation actions that suppliers can put in place where they have caused or contributed to significant environmental impacts.

Table 6. Examples of potential prevention and mitigation activities by suppliers for environmental risks

Environmental issue	Possible corresponding prevention and mitigation actions

Biodiversity loss (e.g. deforestation, coral reef degradation, species loss) and damage to protected areas	In line with the Convention on Biological Diversity (UN, 1992[30]), suppliers may contribute to the conservation of biological diversity, the sustainable use of their components, and the fair and equitable sharing of the benefits arising out of the utilisation of natural resources.
	Suppliers may also avoid and address land, marine and freshwater degradation, including deforestation, in line with objectives of UN SDGs notably 15.2, the UN Strategic Plan for Forests 2017-2030 and the 2021 Glasgow Leaders' Declaration on Forests and Land Use which seek to halt and reverse forest loss and land degradation by 2030.
	Suppliers should prevent and mitigate adverse impacts on biodiversity in national parks, reserves and other protected areas, including UNESCO Natural World Heritage sites, areas protected in fulfilment of the Convention on Biological Diversity, and as defined in domestic law, as well as on protected species. This may include no further exploration, mining, smelting, refining or recycling-related activities in the aforementioned areas as well as environmentally responsible closure of existing exploration, mining, smelting, refining or recycling-related operations.
	Prevention actions
	• Suppliers may ensure that ESIA and ESMP are undertaken to international standards.
	• Where relevant, suppliers may develop a detailed biodiversity action plan to be integrated into management plans.
	• Suppliers may refer to the IFC guidance for PS6 (IFC, 2012[31]) to ensure:
	  o No other viable alternatives within the region exist for development of the project on modified or natural habitats that are not critical.
	  o The project or extractive activities do not lead to measurable adverse impacts on those biodiversity values for which the critical habitat was designated, and on the ecological processes supporting those biodiversity values.
	  o The project does not lead to a net reduction in the global and/or national / regional population of any critically endangered or endangered species over a reasonable period of time.
	  o A robust, appropriately designed, and long-term biodiversity monitoring and evaluation program is integrated into the suppliers management program.
	  o Where such requirements are met, the project's mitigation strategy will be described in a biodiversity action plan integrated into management plans, and will be designed to achieve net gains of those biodiversity values for which the critical habitat was designated.
	• Suppliers and downstream enterprises may use earth observation tools to monitor land-use changes
	• In the context of deep-sea mining, suppliers may consider:
	  o committing to not explore, mine or invest in mining of deep-sea locations where irreversible damage will occur.
	  o conducting scientific studies to confirm that impacts can be mitigated, using realistic measures and are reversible.
	  o obtaining independent confirmation that governance and monitoring of deep-sea mining activities will conform with international good practice.
	Mitigation actions
	• Immediately cease illegal activities.
	• Rehabilitate and restore affected areas.
	• Monitor, quantify and disclose management outcomes.

Environmental issue	Possible corresponding prevention and mitigation actions
	• Efforts to prevent or mitigate adverse impacts on biodiversity should be guided by the biodiversity mitigation hierarchy, which recommends first seeking to avoid damage to biodiversity, reducing or minimising it where avoidance is not possible, and using offsets and restoration as a last resort for adverse impacts that cannot be avoided. Enterprises may plan and implement biodiversity offsetting to address any residual impacts that cannot be avoided and deliver no net loss of biodiversity and ecosystem services (including carbon storage) (OECD, 2016[32]). • Consider applying the World Bank's Bolt-on Forest-Smart ASM Standard and Guidelines for sourcing from ASM in forest landscapes (World Bank, 2019[33]; World Bank, 2021[34]) and the World Bank's Forest Smart Mining Guidance to applying nature-based solutions in the large scale mining sector (World Bank, 2022[35]).
Climate change (e.g. GHG emissions , failure to adapt to physical risks of climate change)	Suppliers should prioritise eliminating or reducing sources of emissions over offsetting, compensation, or neutralization measures. **Prevention actions** • Immediately cease the expansion of any new operations in carbon sinks[1] such as high carbon stock forests or peatlands. • Establish and implement a decarbonization plan in line with internationally agreed global temperature goals and best practices and adopt, implement, monitor and report on short, medium and long-term mitigation targets to ensure credibility and avoid greenwashing. • Establish and implement a climate change adaptation plan to limit the adverse impacts of their operations associated with current and future climate change impacts. **Mitigation actions** • Carbon credits, or offsets may be considered as a means to address unabated emissions as a last resort. Carbon credits or offsets should be of high environmental integrity and should not draw attention away from the need to reduce emissions and should not contribute to avoid locking-in GHG intensive processes and infrastructures.
Improper use and disposal of hazardous materials	The substitution of specific chemicals and materials used along the supply chain can lead to improvements in environmental performance. Substitution or alternatives may be adopted based on their comparative environmental risks, including impact on climate and circularity, life cycle analysis and stakeholder considerations. **Prevention actions** • Gold operations may only use cyanide where the operator is certified by the International Cyanide Management Code (The Cyanide Code, n.d.[36]). **Mitigation actions** • Gold operations can demonstrate progress towards the management and eventual elimination of mercury use by recovering and reusing it. • Gold operations may also participate in a national or local programme to implement the Minamata Convention (UN, 2013[37]) (in the case of ASM) and apply mercury emissions reduction measures in line with the US EPA Mercury Rule (US EPA, n.d.[38]) (in the case of large scale miners).
Noise and vibration	Noise and vibration can be prevented or mitigated by: • Establishing noise and vibration management plans. • Installing noise protection systems. • Improved planning and design of blasting activities. • Noise insulation of equipment and facilities. • Monitoring of noise emissions is a prerequisite for systematic management (EC Joint Research Center, 2021[39]).
Physical and chemical instability	Ensuring physical as well as chemical stability of all mine waste facilities are main long-term objectives of mine waste management to ensure safety of workers and the public as well as preventing leaching of long-term pollutants into the environment. (IGF, 2021[40]) Physical stability of mines can be addressed by: • Backfilling stabilized material into the excavated voids. • Monitoring of physical and chemical stability is a prerequisite to systematic management (EC Joint Research Center, 2021[39]) .
Pollution (air, water, soil)	Activities to prevent and mitigate pollution may include: • Modify facility design to eliminate pollution and the need for treatment of pollution beyond the post-closure monitoring period. • Reduce emissions at source (to the extent possible based on technical limitations). • Implement measures that control emissions related with secondary processing. • Work towards the implementation of appropriate health and safety measures. • Implement measures to capture and treat emissions that cannot be avoided.
Soil erosion and land degradation	Soil erosion and land degradation can be prevented or reduced by: • Establishing erosion and sediment control plans. • Soil management. • Soil conservation measures (EC Joint Research Center, 2021[39]). • Managing runoff with control fences and settling ponds (IGF, 2021[40]).

Environmental issue	Possible corresponding prevention and mitigation actions
Destruction of cultural heritage sites and damage of aesthetics	Activities to prevent and mitigate damage to cultural heritage sites and natural aesthetics may include: • Undertaking an ESIA and ESMP to international standards. • Developing detailed plan to prevent harms to cultural heritage sites. • Anticipating that Indigenous Peoples may expect consultation seeking Free, Prior and Informed Consent (FPIC) and that risks may be generated if such expectations are not met[2]. • Working toward no further exploration, mining, smelting, refining or recycling-related activities within sacred sites or that will irreversibly degrade such sites. • Developing inclusive compensation programmes in consultation with affected stakeholders.
Waste mismanagement	Activities to ensure environmentally responsible Waste management may include: • Working toward reducing and eliminating tailings disposal. • Remediating adverse impacts arising from past disposal of tailings. • Conform with requirements of the Global Industry Standard on Tailings Management for sites generating above a certain threshold of tailings per year. (Global Industry Standard on Tailings Management, 2020[41]).
Water depletion	Actions to prevent and mitigate water depletion may include: • Undertaking an ESIA and ESMP to international standards. • Modifying facility design to implement closed-loop approaches that reduce water consumption and increase water recycling and reuse. • Suppliers in water-stressed areas participating in public-private partnerships to manage water resources sustainably. • Prohibiting water depleting activities where there is high-risk of contributing to water scarcity/diminishing supply of water to cities/settlements. • Create new resources and/or access to ensure no net change in availability and quality of subsistence and traditional resources.
Other	Other activities to support the prevention and mitigation of environmental impacts may include: • Enterprises may demonstrate an anti-corruption policy with environmental protection in scope, and proof of implementation. • Operator may demonstrate progress with implementing a closure plan for mining activities that addresses sudden (unexpected) closure and closure at the end of life-of-mine (including any required long-term maintenance and monitoring) within a reasonable timeframe, backed by adequate financial securities.

1. A carbon sink is anything that absorbs more carbon from the atmosphere than it releases – for example, plants, the ocean and soil. https://www.clientearth.org/latest/latest-updates/stories/what-is-a-carbon-sink/#:~:text=A%20carbon%20sink%20is%20anything,fossil%20fuels%20or%20volcanic%20eruptions .
2. Enterprises should recognise that the process of seeking FPIC as iterative rather than a one-off discussion. Continuous dialogue with the local community will lead to a trust relationship and a balanced agreement that will benefit the enterprise across all phases of the project.

Step 4: Track implementation and results

What does the RBC Guidance say?

- Track the implementation and effectiveness of the enterprise's due diligence activities, i.e. its measures to identify, prevent, mitigate and, where appropriate, support remediation of impacts, including with business relationships.
- Use the lessons learned from tracking to improve due diligence processes in the future.

What additional mineral-specific recommendations are in the Minerals Guidance?

- Monitor and track performance of risk mitigation efforts and report back to designated senior management.
- Carry out independent third-party audit of supply chain due diligence at identified points in the supply chain. Companies at identified points (indicated in the Supplements) should have their due diligence practices audited by independent third parties.

Key questions on how to integrate environmental risk considerations into this step:

- 4.1 How can the tracking of implementation activities and results support the risk-based due diligence process and improve environmental outcomes?
- 4.2 How can an enterprise track the implementation and effectiveness of its own environmental due diligence activities and those of its suppliers? What type of information about environmental risks may be tracked?

4.1 How can the tracking of implementation activities and results support the risk-based due diligence process and improve environmental outcomes?

Enterprises are expected to carry out ongoing monitoring and track progress on the implementation and effectiveness of due diligence against appropriate outcome-oriented and time-bound indicators and targets. Tracking involves first and foremost assessing whether identified adverse impacts have been responded to effectively, prioritising those impacts the enterprise assessed to be most significant under Step 2 and took action to prevent or mitigate under Step 3. How an enterprise tracks the activities and outcomes of prioritised impacts, and how often, will vary according to the context (see question 4.2).

While Steps 2 and 3 will influence the focus of tracking activities, the results or findings from tracking can also inform due diligence and environmental management strategies under Steps 1 and 3. Where objectives and targets are not being met, enterprises can consider whether modifications to the due diligence process, including decisions made with respect to prioritisation, are necessary. This helps to ensure that an enterprises' due diligence is effective, dynamic and adapted to their most severe environmental risks at the time. For example, when seeking to reduce scope 3 GHG emissions, tracking implementation activities and results may identify harder to abate activities in the supply chain or where the enterprise may need to assert more leverage or provide more support and training to achieve targets. Demonstrating continuous and meaningful improvement against appropriate and credible indicators is an important part of tracking. It is also a key characteristic of environmental management systems (see Question 1.3).

4.2 How can an enterprise track the implementation and effectiveness of its own environmental due diligence activities and those of its suppliers? What type of information about environmental risks may be tracked?

To track the implementation and effectiveness of due diligence activities and results effectively, an enterprise will generally need to consider a wide range of information (e.g. assessment data, data from grievance mechanisms or site level visits, desk-top research, and engagement with relevant stakeholders (including workers, workers' representatives and trade unions) and experts). As for other due diligence activities, monitoring and verification should be proportionate and risk-based. How an enterprise tracks the effectiveness of its own due diligence and the due diligence of its suppliers against appropriate targets will depend on the nature, severity and likelihood of the risk (with greater urgency necessary for severe impacts) and on the context, including the nature of its operations, its size and the nature of its business relationships.

For example, if an enterprise is tracking how well it is addressing improper use or disposal of hazardous materials among its prioritised suppliers, it may consider tracking progress both at the site-level (e.g. tracking progress of individual suppliers against correct action plans and tracking specific incidents and how they were handled) and at the global level (e.g. reviewing assessment data, reported grievances and credible reports across relevant high-risk suppliers or geographies). For severe impacts, there is a greater urgency to determine that adverse impacts are being effectively addressed.

Tracking progress on environmental risks and impacts in the supply chain can include, for example:

- **Monitoring the effectiveness of the enterprise's own due diligence activities against its commitments, goals and appropriate indicators**, including evaluating progress on impacts that it may have caused or contributed to and the measures it has taken to support, build capacity, incentivise and otherwise influence its suppliers in the context of their own prevention, mitigation and remediation activities. This can include, for example, monitoring of complaints raised through the enterprise's own operational-level grievance mechanisms or other legitimate remediation mechanisms.[35]
- **Periodic verification and ongoing review of information provided by relevant suppliers on implementation and results of corrective action plans and other due diligence activities.** Enterprises should aim to engage proactively with prioritised suppliers to agree on the most practical and effective way to find and share information on prevention, mitigation and remediation activities and results and to establish the appropriate content, format and frequency of any reporting. Information that might be relevant in a specific context will vary, and will depend on the specific business relationship and other factors, but can include: third party audit reports or other assessment reports, suppliers' public reporting, evidence of site visits and/or stakeholder engagement, information on grievances raised though the suppliers' operational-level grievance mechanism, or other information sources that can inform the enterprise on the status and management of environmental risks and impacts by the supplier.
- **Participating in collaborative initiatives**, including as a means of reducing duplicative assessments and mitigating reporting fatigue for suppliers, and for pooling information, tools and resources.
- **Ongoing and two-way dialogue and open communication between the supplier and the enterprise to monitor progress on prioritised impacts and identify any conditions that may warrant enhanced due diligence**, based on good faith, two-way engagement.
- **Ongoing information-gathering from external sources in order to verify that prioritised risks and adverse impacts have been prevented, mitigated or remediated effectively**, including through meaningful engagement with relevant stakeholders (or their legitimate representatives), desktop research, collaborative approaches or the establishment and regular meetings of supply chain management or environmental working groups or other consultation with experts. See also the case study on independent community monitoring to assess environmental risks below (see Box 4).
- **Technologies such as Geographic Information Systems (GIS), remote sensing, data analytics** and other tools to help track, analyse, alert and notify enterprises further downstream of any issues.

Should the enterprise need to dig deeper into what a supplier is reporting on its due diligence, there are specific data sources that could be requested from or provided by the supplier to facilitate monitoring of implementation and results, as captured in Question 2.2.

Box 7. Independent community monitoring to assess environmental risks

In the context of a specific facility or business activities, community monitoring – also known as citizen science, volunteer environmental monitoring, locally-based monitoring and other related variations – allows communities and business to improve their awareness of environmental risks and impacts and positively influence environmental management outcomes (Danielsen, 2021[42]). Monitoring can be participatory (where the community undertakes monitoring in partnership with the facility or business being monitored) or independent of the facility or business monitoring efforts. Monitoring extends across a wide range of environmental parameters, with water quality, air quality and biodiversity being amongst the most common. Training or other capacity building are frequently required to ensure high-quality environmental data are produced.

The increasing interest in community monitoring has mirrored the rise in participatory decision-making in many jurisdictions and the concept has been well documented (Stepenuck, 2015[43]), particularly in OECD countries (Stepenuck, 2013[44]), but also beyond. It is likely that smartphone apps and online portals will present new opportunities for the continued growth of community monitoring and integration of data in decision-making processes, with new guidance promoting increased uptake.

Although many communities prefer to conduct independent monitoring of adverse impacts of a mine, it is rare that there are enough funds or the will by the local supplier for communities to conduct independent monitoring. Consequently, downstream actors can also support local communities by contributing to independent funds to support this activity and incentivising suppliers to establish community monitoring systems (Sydow et al., 2021[45]).

Step 5: Communicate how impacts are addressed

What does the RBC Guidance say?

- Communicate externally relevant information on due diligence policies, processes, activities conducted to identify and address actual or potential adverse impacts, including the findings and outcomes of those activities.
- Publish information in a way that is easily accessible and appropriate.
- Publish the audit reports of due diligence practices, with due regard taken of business confidentiality and other competitive concerns and responses to identified risks.

Key questions on how to integrate environmental risk considerations into this step:

Questions addressed under this step:

- 5.1 What type of environmental due diligence information can be disclosed by an enterprise? And how can risk-based due diligence support communication activities?
- 5.2. What reporting frameworks already exist that may help enterprises communicate on how environmental risks and impacts in their supply chain are being monitored and addressed

5.1: What type of environmental due diligence information can be disclosed by an enterprise? And how can risk-based due diligence support communication activities?

The RBC Guidance recommends that enterprises' due diligence reporting includes relevant information on measures taken to embed RBC into policies and management systems, the enterprise's identified areas of significant risks and prioritised impacts, prioritisation criteria, actions taken to address priority impacts against targets and their outcomes, measures to track implementation and results, and the provision of or co-operation in any remediation.

Enterprises are expected to take proportionate, risk-based steps to disclose relevant information on their environmental due diligence. This may include information on:

- Any constraints likely to limit the quality or scope of relevant due diligence findings.
- The results of environmental risk assessments and carbon accounting, including significant environmental risks and their receptors, including associated human rights impacts. When communicating information on suppliers' due diligence, information may be shared in aggregate form, or the conditions of reporting agreed with the relevant suppliers.
- Environmental mitigation and remedial measures planned or implemented to address risks or adverse impacts, including details of restoration, remediation, rehabilitation, remedy, partnerships, coalitions and other efforts to build or use leverage.
- Where possible, the results of mitigation and remedial measures.
- Schedule of remedial and monitoring activities.
- Lessons learned and plans for continuous improvement of environmental management and responsible sourcing.

Disclosure of environmental due diligence information is likely to result in responses from impacted or potentially impacted stakeholders and other parties with rights or interests in the process, findings or subsequent monitoring and remediation. This is an opportunity for the enterprise to gather new or additional information that could influence its risk assessment and prioritisation or its mitigation, prevention and remediation planning.

5.2. What reporting frameworks already exist that may help enterprises communicate on how environmental risks and impacts in their supply chain are being monitored and addressed?

There are many reporting frameworks an enterprise can use to help communicate the processes they have in place to address environmental impacts. Some examples of reporting frameworks to help communicate on external environmental impacts are provided below, but enterprises can identify the most suitable reporting frameworks for their needs:

- **The GRI Standards** – particularly GRI 2 General Disclosures (including reporting on the Due Diligence process), GRI 300 series on environmental issues (among others, GRI 308 Supplier Environmental Assessment) https://www.globalreporting.org/how-to-use-the-gri-standards/gri-standards-english-language/
- The **Task Force on Climate-related Financial Disclosures (TCFD)** – particularly the principles for effective disclosures. https://www.fsb-tcfd.org/
- The **Task Force for Nature-Related Financial Disclosures v2.0** – particularly chapter 1 and 2 https://framework.tnfd.global/wp-content/uploads/2022/06/TNFD-Framework-Summary-Executive-Summary-Beta-v0-2.pdf
- **Carbon Disclosure Project (CDP) worldwide** https://www.cdp.net/en
- **GHG protocol** https://ghgprotocol.org/
- **The UN Global Compact** – particularly around guidance on Communication on Progress (CoP). https://unglobalcompact.org/participation/report/cop

- **ISO 14040:2006** – which describes the principles and framework for LCA of specific products, not of the organisation as a whole. This standard addresses environmental impacts in general, including GHG emissions. ISO 14064 provides a standard for the GHG footprint of organizations.

Step 6: Provide for or cooperate in remediation when appropriate

What does the RBC Guidance say?

- When the enterprise identifies that it has **caused or contributed to actual adverse impacts, address such impacts by providing for or cooperating in their remediation**.
- When appropriate, **provide for or cooperate with legitimate remediation mechanisms** through which impacted stakeholders and rightsholders can raise complaints and seek to have them addressed with the enterprise.
- The **appropriate process to enable remediation will be dependent upon several factors** including legal obligations, stakeholder preferences, availability of mechanisms, the nature of the adverse impact and where the adverse impact occurs (i.e. within the enterprise's own operations or its supply chain).

Key questions on how to integrate environmental risk considerations into this step:

- 6.1 What are the different types of remediation relevant to environmental impacts?
- 6.2 How can the mitigation hierarchy support a risk-based approach to environmental remedy? And what can be done in cases where restoration of the environment to its pre-existing condition or rehabilitation of environmental damage is not possible?
- 6.3. What mechanisms and instruments can enable environmental remedy?

6.1: What are the different types of remediation relevant to environmental impacts?

"Remediation" and "remedy" refer to the processes of restoring an affected person or persons (or the environment) to the situation it or they would be in had the adverse impact not occurred. Under the OECD Guidelines there is an expectation that enterprises remediate impacts that they cause or contribute to, or seek to influence remediation by a business relationship where they are directly linked to an impact. In situations of direct linkage, the emphasis is on checking that supplier remediation activities and mechanisms, such as grievance mechanisms, are effective.

In the context of environmental impacts, remedy may take the following forms:

- **Preventative remedy** – puts the focus on activities that prevent or reduce the likelihood of environmental harm happening again. For example, the change of supplier management methods to better identify, monitor and address events that have caused (or are likely to cause) an environmental impact.
- **Restoration and/or rehabilitation practices (sometimes known as primary remediation)** need to be applied, where possible, to re-establish ecosystem structures and functions to a prior state, or a stakeholder agreed end-use state.
- **Compensation of affected stakeholders (sometimes known as compensatory remediation) or offsetting of environmental impacts (sometimes known as complimentary remediation)**. Environmental remediation may be one avenue for achieving remedy for victims of human rights violations through environmental damage. For example, the provision of an alternative water resource.

Examples of common remediation activities associated with environmental impacts include for example:

- **Biodiversity loss** – This might include the restoration, rehabilitation and active protection of damaged or destroyed ecosystems and habitats or bringing back lost species that are found naturally in the area.
- **Water pollution** – Depending on the context and cause of the impact, this might include active or passive water treatment or implementation of reactive barriers to isolate and / or treat contaminated groundwater.
- **Air pollution** – Progressive rehabilitation and implementation of wind barriers on tailings facilities, stockpiles and waste dumps, watering of roads and tracks and implementation of appropriate technologies to reduce emissions.
- **Waste mismanagement** – Clean-up of contaminated soil, through measures that may include bioremediation and / or phytoremediation measures[36].

6.2: How can the mitigation hierarchy support a risk-based approach to environmental remedy? And what can be done in cases where restoration of the environment to its pre-existing condition or rehabilitation of environmental damage is not possible?

Enterprises should prioritise eliminating or reducing environmental harms over offsetting, compensation, or neutralization measures, in line with the principles of the mitigation hierarchy. However, in some cases, it may not be possible to remediate adverse impacts through environmental restoration or rehabilitation measures. In those cases, compensation measures may need to be applied both to nature and to affected rights holders.

Compensation measures in the context of human rights may include financial compensation or relocation of affected rights holders, whereas compensation in an environmental context may include considerations around offsetting and the promotion of restoration in the wider landscape through avoided deforestation and ecosystem degradation.

It is important, however, to carefully evaluate offsets, as there are also social and environmental impacts around the application of offsetting that can be taken into account. For example, in the context of mitigating GHG emissions in an enterprise's supply chain, carbon credits or offsets may be considered as a means to address unabated emissions as a last resort. Furthermore, there is growing policy momentum in favour of the pursuit of both net positive biodiversity outcomes and achieving socio-economic additionalities as part of nature-based solutions, setting expectations of good practice to be beyond offsetting and towards regeneration and the enhancement of natural capital.

6.3. What mechanisms and instruments can enable environmental remedy?

Enterprises participate in remediation for impacts that they cause or contribute to. To participate in remedy, enterprises must establish and participate in mechanisms that allow stakeholders to raise complaints about emerging impacts. These mechanisms may feed into enterprises' ongoing risk prioritisation.

In the case of people who have been impacted by an adverse environmental impact, remedy puts the focus on the victim's right to "equal and effective access to justice; adequate, effective and prompt reparation for harm suffered, and access to relevant information concerning violations and reparation mechanisms." (UN, 2005[46])

Mechanisms to support the provision of environmental remedy may include:

- **Non-judicial mechanisms and operational-level grievance mechanisms** that are legitimate, accessible, predictable, equitable, transparent and dialogue based, including the National Contact Points for RBC.
- **The holding of adequate and secure financial securities** that covers mine reclamation, closure and post-closure activities, maintenance, and monitoring. Establishing **insurance mechanisms** to support environmental remediation and rehabilitation activities or post-mine closure care, as well as addressing damages or liability that may be incurred from activities.
- **Collaborative industry action** to leverage and support remediation activities. Collaborative action can support environmental remedy upstream, particularly in circumstances of cumulative environmental impacts and where remediation activities are more effective when they take place at the landscape level.
- **Legal action (prosecution, litigation and arbitration)** to finance, accelerate and enforce the mechanisms above.

Annex A. Glossary of environmental terms

Biodiversity

Biodiversity means the variability among living organisms from all sources including, inter alia, terrestrial, marine and other aquatic ecosystems and the ecological complexes of which they are part; this includes diversity within species, between species and of ecosystems.

Source: *The Convention on Biological Diversity, Article 2. Use of Terms.* https://www.cbd.int/convention/articles/?a=cbd-02

Critical Habitat

Areas with high biodiversity value, including but not necessarily limited to: (i) habitat of significant importance to critically endangered, endangered species; (ii) habitat of significant importance to endemic and/or restricted range species; (iii) habitat supporting globally significant concentrations of migratory and/or congregatory species; (iv) highly threatened and/or unique ecosystems; and/or (v) areas associated with key evolutionary processes. Other recognized high biodiversity values might also support a critical habitat designation, based on case-by-case evaluation by a specialist.

Source: Adapted from IFC. 2012. Performance Standard 6, Para. 13 and GN55, GN56, 57.

Deep Sea Mining

The process of retrieving mineral deposits from the deep sea – the area of the ocean below 200 m.

Source: International Union for the Conservation of Nature (IUCN). 2020. Issues Brief.

Deforestation

The conversion of forest to other land use independently, whether human-induced or not.

Source: FAO (2020), Global Forest Resources Assessment 2020: Terms and Definitions. https://www.fao.org/3/I8661EN/i8661en.pdf

Ecosystem services

The principal framework for expressing the 'usefulness' of biodiversity is through the concept of ecosystem services. It illustrates the link between, on one hand, the interactions of species with each other and with the physical environment; and on the other, the well-being of people, whether in terms of wealth, nutrition or security. The Millennium Ecosystem Assessment, published in 2005, divided ecosystem services into four categories:

- Provisioning services, or the supply of goods of direct benefit to people, and often with clear monetary value, such as timber from forests, medicinal plants, and fish from the oceans, rivers and lakes.
- Regulating services, the range of functions carried out by ecosystems which are often of great value but generally not given a monetary value in conventional markets. They include regulation of climate through the storing of carbon and control of local rainfall, the removal of pollutants by filtering the air and water, and protection from disasters such as landslides and coastal storms.
- Cultural services, not providing direct material benefits, but contributing to wider needs and desires of society, and therefore to people's willingness to pay for conservation. They include the spiritual value attached to particular ecosystems such as sacred groves, and the aesthetic beauty of landscapes or coastal formations that attract tourists.
- Supporting services, not of direct benefit to people but essential to the functioning of ecosystems and therefore indirectly responsible for all other services. Examples are the formation of soils and the processes of plant growth.

Source: *Convention on Biological Diversity and United Nations Environment Program Factsheet on Ecosystem services* https://www.cbd.int/undb/media/factsheets/undb-factsheet-ecoserv-en.pdf

Free, Prior and Informed Consent

People are (i) 'not coerced, pressured or intimidated in their choices of development'; (ii) 'their consent is sought and freely given prior to authorisation of development activities'; (iii) they 'have full information about the scope and impacts of the proposed development activities on their lands, resources and wellbeing'; and (iv) 'their choice to give or withhold consent over developments affecting them is respected and upheld'

Source: UN Permanent Forum on Indigenous Issues (UNPFII, 2005:12).

Forest

Land spanning more than 0.5 hectares with trees higher than 5 meters and a canopy cover of more than 10%, or trees able to reach these thresholds in situ. It does not include land that is predominantly under agricultural or urban land use.

Source: FAO (2020), Global Forest Resources Assessment 2020: Terms and Definitions. https://www.fao.org/3/I8661EN/i8661en.pdf

Greenhouse Gases (GHG)

Greenhouse gases are those gaseous constituents of the atmosphere, both natural and anthropogenic, that absorb and emit radiation at specific wavelengths within the spectrum of terrestrial radiation emitted by the earth's surface, the atmosphere itself, and by clouds. This property causes the greenhouse effect. Water vapour (H2O), carbon dioxide (CO2), nitrous oxide (N2O), methane (CH4) and ozone (O3) are the primary greenhouse gases in the earth's atmosphere. Moreover, there are a number of entirely human-made greenhouse gases in the atmosphere, such as the halocarbons and other chlorine- and bromine- containing substances, dealt with under the Montreal Protocol. Beside CO2, N2O and CH4, the Kyoto Protocol deals with the greenhouse gases sulphur hexafluoride (SF6), hydrocarbons (HFCs), nitrogen triflouride (NF3), and perfluorocarbons (PFCs)

Source: Intergovernmental Panel on Climate Change (IPCC). 2014. Climate Change 2014: Mitigation of Climate Change. Contribution of Working Group III to the Fifth Assessment Report of the Intergovernmental Panel on Climate Change.

High Conservation Value (HCV)

Biological, ecological, social or cultural values considered outstandingly significant at the national, regional or global level.

Source: UNEP WCMC Biodiversity A to Z.

Just transition

A concept originally introduced in the UNFCCC Paris Agreement (2015) where a key Guiding principle of the Agreement is for countries to "take into account the imperatives of a just transition of the workforce and the creation of decent work and quality jobs in accordance with nationally defined development priorities."

The OECD Guidelines for Multinational Enterprises on Responsible Business Conduct note that carrying out environmental due diligence and managing adverse environmental impacts will often involve taking into account multiple environmental, social and developmental priorities. In this respect it is important for enterprises to assess and address social impacts in the context of their environmental management and due diligence activities and to take action to prevent and mitigate such adverse impacts both in their transition away from environmentally harmful practices, as well as towards greener industries or practices, such as the use of renewable energy.

Source: OECD (2023), OECD Guidelines for Multinational Enterprises on Responsible Business Conduct, OECD Publishing, Paris, https://doi.org/10.1787/81f92357-en.

Key Biodiversity Area

Sites contributing significantly to the global persistence of biodiversity, in terrestrial, freshwater and marine ecosystems. They represent the most important sites for biodiversity conservation worldwide and are identified nationally using globally standardised criteria and thresholds.

Source: UNEP WCMC, modified from IUCN. 2016. Global Standard for the Identification of Key Biodiversity Areas.

Life Cycle Assessment (LCA)

Compilation and evaluation of the inputs, outputs and the potential environmental impacts of a product or service throughout its life cycle.

Source: Intergovernmental Panel on Climate Change (IPCC). 2018. Special Report on Global Warming of 1.5°C – SR15, modified from ISO, 2018: ISO 14044:2006.

Mitigation Hierarchy

"The mitigation hierarchy is a set of prioritized steps to alleviate environmental (or social) harm as far as possible through avoidance, minimization and restoration of adverse impacts. Compensation/offsetting are only considered to address residual impacts after appropriate avoidance, minimization and restoration measures have been applied. The biodiversity mitigation hierarchy is as follows (but the steps can be applied for any environmental or social impacts):

i. Avoidance: measures taken to avoid creating impacts from the outset, such as careful spatial or temporal placement of elements of infrastructure, in order to completely avoid impacts on certain components of biodiversity. This results in a change to a 'business as usual' approach.
ii. Minimization: Measures taken to reduce the duration, intensity and/or extent of impacts that cannot be completely avoided, as far as is practically feasible.
iii. Restoration: measures taken to assist the recovery of ecosystems that have been degraded, damaged or destroyed. Involves altering an area in such a way as to re-establish an ecosystem's composition, structure and function, usually bringing it back to its original (pre-disturbance) state or to a healthy state close to the original.
iv. Offset: Measurable conservation outcomes resulting from actions designed to compensate for significant residual adverse impacts on biodiversity arising from project development after appropriate prevention and mitigation actions have been taken. The goal of biodiversity offsets is no net loss or a net gain of biodiversity on the ground with respect to species composition, habitat structure, ecosystem function and people's use and cultural values associated with biodiversity."

Source: Initiative for Responsible Mining Assurance (IRMA). 2018. Standard Glossary of Terms.

Nature-based solutions

Nature-based solutions are measures that protect, sustainably manage or restore nature, with the goal of maintaining or enhancing ecosystem services to address a variety of social, environmental and economic challenges.

Source: OECD (2020), *Nature-based solutions for adapting to water-related climate risks*. Policy Perspectives. OECD Environment Policy Paper No. 21. OECD Publishing. Paris, *https://doi.org/10.1787/2257873d-en*.

Natural capital

Nature is an asset or capital stock (i.e. natural capital), like produced (physical) and human capital. Natural capital provides goods and services that contribute directly or indirectly to a country's economic output and human well-being. But it is much more than an economic good; nature also holds intrinsic value. Natural capital is the most important of all capital stocks, as it provides fundamental life-support functions. It sets the ecological boundaries for socio-economic systems.

Source: OECD (2021), *Biodiversity, Natural Capital and the Economy: A Policy Guide for Finance, Economic and Environment Ministers*. Policy Perspectives. OECD Environment Policy Paper NO. 26. OECD Publishing. Paris. https://www.oecd-ilibrary.org/docserver/1a1ae114-en.pdf?expires=1693395607&id=id&accname=ocid84004878&checksum=43C12709219D3FDDEE2CA8FC7E142008.

Offsets

- **Biodiversity Offsets** Biodiversity offsets are measurable conservation outcomes that result from actions designed to compensate for significant, residual biodiversity loss from development projects. They are intended to be implemented only after reasonable steps have been taken to avoid and minimise biodiversity loss at a development site. Biodiversity offsets are based on the premise that impacts from development can be compensated for if sufficient habitat can be protected, enhanced or established elsewhere. Biodiversity offsets are economic instruments and are based on the polluter pays approach. They aim to internalise the external costs of biodiversity loss from development projects by imposing a cost on the activities that cause adverse impacts to biodiversity.

Source: OECD (2016), *Biodiversity Offsets: Effective Design and Implementation*, Policy Highlights. OECD Publishing, Paris https://www.oecd.org/environment/resources/Policy-Highlights-Biodiversity-Offsets-web.pdf

- **Carbon or GHG Offsets** A carbon offset is a reduction in emissions of carbon dioxide or other greenhouse gases made in order to compensate for ("offset") an emission made elsewhere.

Source: https://www.ipcc.ch/2018/06/15/ipcc-meetings-go-carbon-neutral/#:~:text=A%20carbon%20offset%20is%20a,%E2%80%9D)%20an%20emission%20made%20elsewhere.

Protected Area

"A clearly defined geographical space, recognized, dedicated and managed, through legal or other effective means, to achieve the long-term conservation of nature with associated ecosystem services and cultural values." The definition is expanded by six "protected area management categories" covering strict nature reserve, wilderness area, national park, natural monument or feature, habitat / species management area, protected landscape or seascape.

Source: Modified from Dudley (2008), Guidelines for Applying Protected Area Management Categories. International Union for the Conservation of Nature (IUCN).

Reclamation

The process of making severely degraded land fit for cultivation or a state suitable for some human use.

Source: Society for Ecological Restoration's international standards.

Rehabilitation

Measures taken to rehabilitate degraded ecosystems or cleared ecosystems following exposure to impacts that cannot be completely avoided and/ or minimised. Rehabilitation emphasizes the reparation of ecosystem processes, productivity and services. Rehabilitation cannot always restore the ecosystem to its pre-existing condition, but it aims at re-establishing species and communities of the ecosystem.

Source: Modified from BBOP & UNEP. 2010. Mitigation Hierarchy. Business and Biodiversity Offsets Programme & United Nations Environment Programme, Washington DC, USA; BBOP. 2012. Glossary. Business and Biodiversity Offsets Programme, Washington DC, USA.

Restoration

Re-establishment of ecosystem structure and function to an image of its prior near-natural state or replication of a desired reference ecosystem.

Source: International Council on Mining and Metals (ICMM). 2019. Integrated mine closure: Good practice guide (2nd ed.)

Scope 1, 2 and 3 emissions

Emissions responsibility as defined by the GHG Protocol, a private sector initiative. 'Scope 1' indicates direct GHG emissions that are from sources owned or controlled by the reporting entity. 'Scope 2' indicates indirect GHG emissions associated with the production of electricity, heat, or steam purchased by the reporting entity. 'Scope 3' indicates all other indirect emissions, i.e. emissions associated with the extraction and production of purchased materials, fuels, and services, including transport in vehicles not owned or controlled by the reporting entity, outsourced activities, waste disposal, etc.

Source: Intergovernmental Panel on Climate Change (IPCC). 2014. Climate Change 2014: Mitigation of Climate Change, modified from WBCSD and WRI, 2004.

Annex B. Non-exhaustive list of tools to identify, assess and manage environmental risks and impacts

Accountability, ratings and disclosure

- AA1000 AccountAbility Principles
- GRI Standards: 101 Foundation and 102 General Disclosures
- Task Force for Nature Financial Disclosures v2.0 (TNFD) and its Glossary of Key Terms
- Task Force on Climate-Related Financial Disclosures (TCFD)
- Carbon Disclosure Project (CDP)
- Ecovadis
- Institutional Shareholder Services (ISS)
- MSCI
- Sustainalytics
- Dow Jones Sustainability Indices (DJSI)

Best Available Techniques (BAT) reference documents (BREFs) – for example

- Production of Cement, Lime and Magnesium Oxide – BREF BATC (04.2013)
- Emissions from Storage – BREF (07.2006)
- Energy Efficiency – BREF (02.2009)
- Ferrous Metals Processing Industry – BREF (12.2001)
- Industrial Cooling Systems – BREF (12.2001)
- Iron and Steel Production – BREF BATC (03.2012)
- Non-ferrous Metals Industries – BREF BATC (06.2016)
- Refining of Mineral Oil and Gas – BREF BATC (10.2014)
- Waste Treatment – BREF BATC (08.2018)
- Manufacture of Glass – BREF BATC (03.2012)
- Ceramic Manufacturing Industry – BREF (08.2007)

Biodiversity

- Good Practice Guide for Mining and Biodiversity
- Integrated Biodiversity Assessment Tool (IBAT)

Community and stakeholder engagement

- IHRB Promoting Human Rights and Ensuring Social Inclusion in the Extractives Sector.
- IFC Stakeholder Engagement Practice Handbook
- AA1000 Stakeholder Engagement Standard

- OECD Due Diligence Guidance for Meaningful Stakeholder Engagement in the Extractive Sector

Greenhouse gas emissions

- GHG Protocol

Impact Assessment

- IFC Performance Standard 1. Social and Environmental Assessment and Management Systems
- WBCSD Cement Sustainability Initiative Guidelines for Environmental & Social Impact Assessment.
- International Council on Mining and Metals (ICMM) Good Practice Guidance on Health Impact Assessment
- IAIA The Circular Economy and Impact Assessment - A Primer
- IAIA The State of Digital Impact Assessment Practice
- IFC Good Practice Handbook - Cumulative Impact Assessment and Management: Guidance for the Private Sector in Emerging Markets

Life Cycle Assessment (LCA)

- ISO 14040 Environmental management – Life cycle assessment – Principles and framework
- Ecoinvent Database

Risk Assessment and Management.

- ISO 31000 – Risk management

Tailings management

- Global Industry Standard on Tailings
- Guidelines for Responsible Mine Tailings

Water management

- UNEP Integrated Water Resources Management
- UNESCO World Water Assessment Programme
- AWS International Water Stewardship Standard
- CEO Water Mandate's Water Disclosure Guidelines
- Aqueduct Water Risk Atlas (wri.org)

Grievance mechanisms, incident reporting and monitoring

- International Council on Mining and Metals (ICMM), Handling and Resolving Local-level Concerns and Grievances: Human rights in the mining and metals sector
- Kufatilia ("to track" in Swahili) is an SMS-based platform to support incident reporting and monitoring through the work of a network of Civil Society Organisations in Eastern DRC.

Remedy and/or remediation

- Basic Principles and Guidelines on the Right to a Remedy and Reparation for Victims of Gross Violations of International Human Rights Law and Serious Violations of International Humanitarian Law

Relevant initiatives

- Towards Sustainable Mining
- The Raw Materials Outlook Platform
- The Materials Insight
- Water Resilience Coalition

References

Bibas, R., J. Chateau and E. Lanzi (2021), *Policy scenarios for a transition to a more resource efficient and circular economy*, https://doi.org/10.1787/c1f3c8d0-en. [8]

Danielsen, F. (2021), "The Concept, Practice, Application, and Results of Locally Based Monitoring of the Environment", *BioScience*, Vol. 71/5, pp. 484-502, https://doi.org/10.1093/biosci/biab021. [42]

EC Joint Research Center (2021), *Collection of available techniques for the prevention or reduction of environmental impacts in non-energy extractive industries (NEEI)*, https://publications.jrc.ec.europa.eu/repository/handle/JRC125247 (accessed on 2023). [39]

European Union (2021), *Capacity4Dev: Strategic Environmental Assessment.* [23]

Garbarino, E. et al. (2021), *Collection of available techniques for the prevention or reduction of environmental impacts in non-energy extractive industries (NEEI), EUR 30827 EN, Publications Office of the European Union, Luxembourg.* [18]

Global Industry Standard on Tailings Management (2020), , https://globaltailingsreview.org/ (accessed on 2023). [41]

IAIA (n.d.), *International Association of Impact Assessment*, https://www.iaia.org/uploads/pdf/Fastips_18%20Scoping.pdf (accessed on 2023). [22]

IBAT Alliance (n.d.), *Integrated Biodiversity Assessment Tool*, https://www.ibat-alliance.org/ (accessed on 2023). [21]

IEA (2021), *The Role of Critical Minerals in Clean Energy Transitions.* [3]

IFC (2013), *Cumulative Impact Assessment and Management: Guidance for the Private Sector in Emerging Markets*, https://www.ifc.org/wps/wcm/connect/58fb524c-3f82-462b-918f-0ca1af135334/IFC_GoodPracticeHandbook_CumulativeImpactAssessment.pdf?MOD=AJPERES&CVID=kbnYgI5 (accessed on 2023). [14]

IFC (2012), *Biodiversity Conservation and Sustainable Management of Living Natural Resources*, https://www.ifc.org/en/insights-reports/2012/ifc-performance-standard-6 (accessed on 2023). [31]

IGF (2021), *Guidance for Governments: Environmental management and Environmental management and*, https://www.igfmining.org/resource/guidance-for-governments-environmental-management-and-mining-governance/ (accessed on 2023). [40]

IGF (2017), *Global Trends in Artisanal and Small-Scale Mining (ASM): A Review of Key Numbers and Issues*, IISD, https://www.iisd.org/system/files/publications/igf-asm-global-trends.pdf. [10]

Lead Recycling Africa Project (2016), *Findings from Lead Recycling Africa Project*, https://www.oeko.de/oekodoc/2549/2016-076-de.pdf. [25]

Maddox, T. et al. (2019), *Forest-Smart Mining: Identifying Factors Associated with the Impacts of Large-Scale Mining on Forests*. [47]

Moore, K. et al. (2020), "The re-direction of small deposit mining: Technological solutions for raw materials supply security in a whole systems context", *Resources, Conservation & Recycling*, Vol. 7, https://doi.org/10.1016/j.rcrx.2020.100040. [11]

OECD (2023), *OECD Guidelines for Multinational Enterprises on Responsible Business Conduct*, OECD Publishing, Paris, https://doi.org/10.1787/81f92357-en. [16]

OECD (2021), *Costs and Value of Due Diligence in Mineral Supply Chains - OECD Position*, https://mneguidelines.oecd.org/costs-and-value-of-due-diligence-in-mineral-supply-chains.pdf. [49]

OECD (2021), *Policy scenarios for a transition to a more resource efficient and circular economy*, https://doi.org/10.1787/19970900. [5]

OECD (2021), *The role of OECD instruments on responsible business conduct in progressing environmental objectives*, https://mneguidelines.oecd.org/The-role-of-OECD-instruments-on-responsible-business-conduct-in-progressing-environmental-objectives.pdf. [7]

OECD (2021), *Trends in Stakeholder Reporting: Mineral Supply Chains*, https://mneguidelines.oecd.org/trendsinstakeholderreportingmineralsupplychains.htm. [13]

OECD (2020), *Environment at a Glance 2020*, https://doi.org/10.1787/19964064. [4]

OECD (2019), *Business Models for the Circular Economy: Opportunities and Challenges for Policy*,, https://doi.org/10.1787/g2g9dd62-en. [6]

OECD (2019), *Global Material Resources Outlook to 2060*, https://doi.org/10.1787/9789264307452-en. [2]

OECD (2019), *Global Material Resources Outlook to 2060: Economic Drivers and Environmental consequences*, https://doi.org/10.1787/9789264307452-en. [17]

OECD (2018), *OECD Due Diligence Guidance for Responsible Business Conduct*, OECD, https://mneguidelines.oecd.org/OECD-Due-Diligence-Guidance-for-Responsible-Business-Conduct.pdf. [15]

OECD (2017), *OECD Due Diligence Guidance for Meaningful Stakeholder Engagement in the Extractive Sector*, https://doi.org/10.1787/9789264252462-en. [48]

OECD (2016), *Biodiversity Offsets: Effective Design and Implementation*, https://doi.org/10.1787/9789264222519-en. [32]

OECD (2016), *FAQ on Sourcing Gold from Artisanal and Small-Scale Miners*, http://mneguidelines.oecd.org/FAQ_Sourcing-Gold-from-ASM-Miners.pdf. [12]

OECD (2016), *OECD Due Diligence Guidance for Responsible Supply Chains of Minerals from Conflict-Affected and High-Risk Areas: Third Edition*, OECD Publishing, Paris, https://doi.org/10.1787/9789264252479-en. [24]

OECD (1996), *OECD GUIDELINES FOR TESTING OF CHEMICALS. PROPOSAL FOR UPDATING GUIDELINE 305. Bioconcentration: Flow-through Fish Test*, https://www.oecd.org/env/ehs/testing/E305_Fish%20Bioaccumulation.pdf. [50]

SER (n.d.), *International Responsible Business Agreement for the Metals Sector*, https://www.imvoconvenanten.nl/en/metals-sector/convenant (accessed on 2023). [28]

Stepenuck, K. (2015), "Individual- and community-level impacts of volunteer environmental monitoring: a synthesis of peer-reviewed literature", *Ecology and Society*, Vol. 20/3, https://doi.org/10.5751/ES-07329-200319. [43]

Stepenuck, K. (2013), *Improving understanding of outcomes and credibility of volunteer environmental monitoring programs. Dissertation. University of Wisconsin–Madison, Madison, Wisconsin, USA.*. [44]

Sydow, J. et al. (2021), *Environmental responsibility through supply chains: Insights from Latin America.*. [45]

The Cyanide Code (n.d.), , https://cyanidecode.org/ (accessed on 2023). [36]

UN (2022), *A/76/L.75, The human right to a clean, healthy and sustainable environment : draft resolution*, https://digitallibrary.un.org/record/3982508?ln=en. [29]

UN (2013), *Minamata Convention on Mercury*, https://mercuryconvention.org/en/documents/minamata-convention-mercury-text-and-annexes (accessed on 2023). [37]

UN (2005), *Resolution 60/147 Basic Principles and Guidelines on the Right to a Remedy and Reparation for Victims of Gross Violations of International Human Rights Law and Serious Violations of International Humanitarian Law*, https://www.ohchr.org/en/instruments-mechanisms/instruments/basic-principles-and-guidelines-right-remedy-and-reparation. [46]

UN (1992), *Convention on Biological Diversity*, https://www.cbd.int/convention/text/. [30]

UNEP (2022), *How disposable tech is feeding an e-waste crisis*, https://www.unep.org/news-and-stories/story/how-disposable-tech-feeding-e-waste-crisis. [26]

UNEP (2019), *Gloabl Resources Outlook 2019*, https://www.resourcepanel.org/reports/global-resources-outlook. [51]

UNEP (n.d.), *E-WASTE 2.0*, https://wedocs.unep.org/bitstream/handle/20.500.11822/7587/c_waste_infog_en.pdf?sequence=5&amp%3BisAllowed=y%2C%20Chinese%7C%7Chttps%3A//wedocs.unep.org/bitstream/handle/20.500.11822/7587/-E-waste_20_Recycling_for_sustainability-2016E-waste_infog_zh.pdf.p (accessed on 2023). [27]

UNISDR (2008), *Developing Early Warnin Systems: A Checklist: EWC III Third international Conference on Early Warning 27-29 March 2006 at Bonn, Germany*, https://www.unisdr.org/files/608_10340.pdf (accessed on 2023). [19]

United Nations Framework Convention on Climate Change (2016), *Decision 1/CP.21 Adoption* [1] *of the Paris Agreement FCCC/CP/2015/10/Add.1, par. 133,,* https://undocs.org/en/FCCC/CP/2015/10/Add.1.

US EPA (n.d.), *Mercury Specific Laws and Regulation*. [38]

World Bank (2022), *Forest-Smart Mining : Guidance to Applying Nature-Based Solutions in the Large-Scale Mining Sector*, https://policycommons.net/artifacts/2419759/forest-smart-mining/3441396/ (accessed on 2023). [35]

World Bank (2021), *Developing Forest-Smart Artisanal and Small-Scale Mining (ASM) Standards*. [34]

World Bank (2020), *Minerals for Climate Action: The Mineral Intensity of the Clean Energy Transition*, https://pubdocs.worldbank.org/en/961711588875536384/Minerals-for-Climate-Action-The-Mineral-Intensity-of-the-Clean-Energy-Transition. [9]

World Bank (2019), *Forest-Smart Mining: Identifying Factors Associated with the Impacts of Large-Scale Mining on Forests*, https://openknowledge.worldbank.org/entities/publication/55579809-e147-5c25-a222-d976a8fac8db (accessed on 2023). [33]

World Resources Institute (2021), *Aqueduct Water Risk Atlas*, https://www.wri.org/data/aqueduct-water-risk-atlas. [20]

Notes

[1] There is no definitive list of minerals critical to the energy and digital transitions, and a mineral's assessed criticality can change over time and between countries.

[2] For more information see OECD (2023), Net Zero+: Climate and Economic Resilience in a Changing World, OECD Publishing, Paris, https://doi.org/10.1787/da477dda-en.

[3] A sub-set of upstream entities located at or immediately around the point of transformation like smelters, refiners and international concentrate traders are sometimes referred to as 'mid-stream' to distinguish them from other upstream entities.

[4] This includes climate litigation, with the 2021 judgement by the District Court of the Netherlands highlighting the role of the OECD Guidelines for MNEs in understanding the duty of care owed by business on climate action and emissions reduction obligations: Milieudefensie et al. v. Royal Dutch Shell plc, https://uitspraken.rechtspraak.nl/inziendocument?id=ECLI: NL: RBDHA:2021:5339.

5 Non-party Stakeholders under the United Nations Framework Convention on Climate Change include national governments, cities, regions and other sub national entities, international organizations, civil society, indigenous peoples, women, youth, academic institutions, as well as businesses) acting as individual entities or in partnerships.

[6] See Part I of OECD's Global Material Resources Outlook to 2060: Economic Drivers and Environmental Consequences (OECD, 2019[2]) or Chap 2.1 of UNEP's Global Resources Outlook (UNEP, 2019[51]).

[7] It is important to note that circular economy approaches can be applied at all stages of the minerals supply chain, including extraction. For example, the recovery of minerals from extractive waste rather than reverting to landfill or the reuse/recycling of equipment.

[8] For more information and resources on Human rights and the environment, please see the website of the OHCHR's Special Rapporteur on human rights and the environment, https://www.ohchr.org/en/special-procedures/sr-environment.

[9] Product design and production processes of downstream enterprises are also crucial for sustainable development as product design and the choice of materials used in production determine the type of products that enter the market as well as how recyclable these products are.

[10] This issue is explored further in the OECD Position Paper on Costs and Value of Due Diligence in Mineral Supply Chains (OECD, 2021[50]).

[11] Adverse environmental impacts specifically referenced in the MNE Guidelines are not exhaustive. Other related and more specific impacts were identified by the expert working group for the Handbook.

[12] See the Glossary for more information on Biodiversity.

[13] Subject to evolving interpretation, indirect impacts can be treated as contribution or direct linkage under RBCs involvement framework, depending on specific circumstances.

[14] See the RBC Guidance, Annex, Q3 for meanings of these terms.

[15] See the Glossary for more information on Scope 1, 2 and 3 emissions.

[16] Under OECD RBC standards, the severity of a risk or impact is determined according to its scale, scope and irremediable character. See RBC Guidance, Annex, Question 3, p. 42.

[17] For a deeper analysis on the risk-based approach, readers can refer to the Background note on Regulatory Developments concerning Due Diligence for Responsible Business Conduct and the background note on Translating a risk-based due diligence approach into law, developed by the OECD Secretariat.

[18] See the Glossary for a more detailed explanation of the mitigation hierarchy.

[19] For best practice on gender responsive due diligence, see the Gender-Responsive Due Diligence Platform (https://www.genderduediligence.org/), the US Department of State Fact Sheet Managing Risks to Women in Supply Chains (https://www.state.gov/managing-risks-to-women-in-supply-chains/), and the working group Women's Rights and Mining (https://womenandmining.org/) .

[20] Under OECD RBC standards, relevant stakeholders are understood as persons or groups, or their legitimate representatives, who have rights or interests related to the matters covered by the Guidelines that are or could be affected by adverse impacts associated with the enterprise's operations, products or services (MNE Guidelines, Commentary, Chapter II, paragraph 28 and RBC Guidance, Annex, Q.8, p. 48).

[21] For example, see the Commentary to the Commentary on Chapter II: General Policies of the OECD Guidelines for Multinational Enterprises on Responsible Business Conduct (OECD, 2023[16]). For more information on stakeholder engagement in the extractives sector, please see OECD Due Diligence Guidance for Meaningful Stakeholder Engagement in the Extractive Sector (OECD, 2017[49]): https://mneguidelines.oecd.org/stakeholder-engagement-extractive-industries.htm.

[22] For example, building upon guidance in existing ASM standards, such as Fairtrade, Fairmined, the Code of Risk-mitigation for artisanal and small-scale mining engaging in Formal Trade (CRAFT Code), Planet GOLD+, Gemfair, the World Bank's Forest Smart ASM Bolt-on Standard, and so on.

[23] These include the following:

Sector risks are risks that are prevalent within a sector globally as a result of the characteristics of the sector, its activities, its products and production processes. For example, the extractive sector is often associated with risks related to a large environmental footprint and impacts on local communities.

Product risks are risks related to inputs or production processes used in the development or use of specific products. For example, phones and computers may contain components that are at risk of being mined from conflict areas.

Geographic risks are conditions in a particular country which may make sector risks more likely. Geographic risk factors can generally be classified as those related to the regulatory framework (e.g. alignment with international conventions), governance (e.g. strength of inspectorates, rule of law, level of corruption), socio-economic context (e.g. poverty and education rates, vulnerability and discrimination of specific populations) and political context (e.g. presence of conflict).

Enterprise-level risks are risks associated with a specific enterprise such as weak governance, a poor history of conduct in relation to respecting human rights, labour rights, anti-corruption standards, environmental standards, or a lack of culture around RBC.

[24] For example, The World Bank's Forest Smart Mining reports on LSM (Maddox et al., 2019[47]) and the Artisanal and Small-Scale Mining Bolt-on Standard (World Bank, 2021[34]) both provide a useful set of criteria and indicators for assessing the extent to which a mining operation is managing its risks to forest values.

[25] Examples include UNEP's Map-X (Projects – MapX) and ASM Spotter: https://www.mapx.org/projects/.

[26] For more information on the role of sustainability initiatives in due diligence, see the Background note on regulatory developments: The role of sustainability initiatives in mandatory due diligence: http://mneguidelines.oecd.org/the-role-of-sustainability-initiatives-in-mandatory-due-diligence-note-for-policy-makers.pdf Further information on the OECD's Alignment Assessments of sustainability initiatives, including in the minerals sector, is available here: https://www.oecd.org/corporate/industry-initiatives-alignment-assessment.htm.

[27] Safety data sheets are a mechanism for transmitting appropriate safety information on substances and mixtures whish are, for example meet criteria for classification as hazardous or a substance is persistent, bioaccumulative and toxic. (https://echa.europa.eu/documents/10162/2324906/sds_en.pdf/01c29e23-2cbe-49c0-aca7-72f22e101e20).

[28] Bioconcentration/bioaccumulation is the increase in concentration of the test substance in or on an organism (specified tissues thereof) relative to the concentration of test substance in the surrounding medium. (OECD, 1996[51])

[29] The ability of a substance to cause deleterious effects to living organisms during a long-term exposure. https://www.sciencedirect.com/topics/agricultural-and-biological-sciences/chronic-toxicity

[30] A "landscape approach" is a term used to describe collaborative initiatives in specific places that span multiple sectors and go beyond the scale of individual farms, forest management units and protected areas. It is a coherent intervention at a landscape scale to secure food, fibre and energy production, improvements in social welfare, water security and ecosystem conservation. http://forestsolutions.panda.org/solutions/landscape-approaches

[31] While mine-closure and post mining plans are rarely established and implemented by ASM, this Handbook provides considerations for progressive engagement on this difficult issue.

[32] For more information please see p80-81 of the RBC Guidance.

[33] Severity is not an absolute concept and is context-specific; where the risk of a potential impact is most likely and most severe will be specific to the enterprise, its sector and the nature of its business relationships. Severity is determined according to three factors, set out in the RBC Guidance:

- Scale: the gravity or seriousness of the potential or actual impact, such as the degree of serious impact on workers' health and safety, degree of waste or chemical generation; or loss of life or severe bodily harm caused.
- Scope: the reach or extent of the potential or actual impact, for example the number of individuals that are or will be affected, or the extent of environmental damage or other environmental impact.
- Irremediable character: its irreversible nature, or any limits on the ability to restore the individuals or environment affected to a situation equivalent to their situation before the adverse impact.

[34] See Glossary for key definitions.

[35] See Step 6 of the RBC Guidance and Annex, Q.48-54.

[36] The use of microorganisms (bioremediation) or plants (phytoremediation) to remediate soils following contamination.

www.ingramcontent.com/pod-product-compliance
Lightning Source LLC
Chambersburg PA
CBHW061224240926
51846CB00006B/1351
* 9 7 8 9 2 6 4 5 2 2 0 6 0 *